On Conquering Schizophrenia

From the Desk of a Therapist and Survivor

With Purview on Metaphysics, Philosophy, and Theology

by ROBERT FRANCIS

"*dawn recreates, hope restores*"
"*with wings, follows essense*"

ON CONQUERING SCHIZOPHRENIA
FROM THE DESK OF A THERAPIST AND SURVIVOR

Copyright © 2019 Robert Francis.

All rights reserved. No part of this book may be used or reproduced by any means, graphic, electronic, or mechanical, including photocopying, recording, taping or by any information storage retrieval system without the written permission of the author except in the case of brief quotations embodied in critical articles and reviews.

iUniverse books may be ordered through booksellers or by contacting:

iUniverse
1663 Liberty Drive
Bloomington, IN 47403
www.iuniverse.com
1-800-Authors (1-800-288-4677)

Because of the dynamic nature of the Internet, any web addresses or links contained in this book may have changed since publication and may no longer be valid. The views expressed in this work are solely those of the author and do not necessarily reflect the views of the publisher, and the publisher hereby disclaims any responsibility for them.

Any people depicted in stock imagery provided by Getty Images are models, and such images are being used for illustrative purposes only.
Certain stock imagery © Getty Images.

ISBN: 978-1-5320-6990-1 (sc)
ISBN: 978-1-5320-6989-5 (e)

Library of Congress Control Number: 2019904123

Print information available on the last page.

iUniverse rev. date: 04/18/2019

Epigraph-

[A]affliction produces endurance, and endurance, proven character, and proven character, hope, and hope does not disappoint.

—*Letter to the Romans 5:3-5*

Introduction

To you, my dear reader:

Inspiration is essential to the creative process, including excellent writing. But of what etiology does inspiration spring? Inspiration is not simply handed to you with explicit instructions to proceed with a creative excellence. Rather, inspiration can be elusive, for its tappable source often resides in murky psychological depths. Inspiration often follows personal hardship. Some of the greatest creative works flow from melancholy, angst, psychological agitation, and from the dark recesses of troubled minds. A personal familiarity with the dark night has been known to impel inspired intellectual and artistic creation. On the other hand, the happy and well-adjusted too can lay claim of illumined inspiration, for from a joyful countenance works of brilliance are known too to follow. In my particular instance, for the impetus to this book, my inspiration was two-fold and it entails contributory ingredients from both typical sources.

First, of the lighted. My first inspiration to write this book came from the encouragement of one of the most good and decent human beings ever to traverse this earth. And because of such a deep respect, adoration, and love, I austerely call this individual Mom. There is nothing dark about this etiology. It is pure, and it is good. Mom always urged me to write and without this encouragement this book would have never become tangible. I was captive to my perceived limitations of being incapable of quality authorship. Mom had very little doubt however and over the course of three decades would remind me occasionally of this perceived talent. So, I thank Mom, whose heart is gold and customarily filled with a most wholesome type of undeniable cheer.

Second, of the darkened. The second etiology of inspiration for this authorship indeed flows from psychological darkness. Schizophrenia can be highly casual to a dark and agitated mind. This darkness contained in the schizophrenic mind can be like a visual cyclonic whirlwind and an auditory atonal cacophony of unrelenting insane ideas that caustically impugn any sense of a rational centeredness. Schizophrenia produces psychological content of a repugnant rational disregard and does so with a rapacious indignation. It is from this dark source, the disease of schizophrenia, that an undeniable light penetrated my otherwise darkened mind with a pointed inspiration to a felt literary compulsion. I suppose this may not instill a sense of cheery optimism as you leap into the content of this book. But, please, heed not my dear reader, for I offer you firm assurance that over the course of this literary journey you will sense an ethereal quality with tinges of a felt abdominal humor that will provide ample psychological shelter and an affluent emotional repose. Our destination, however, will only be reached with a little persistence and with a dash and sprinkle of an essential faith.

From foreword to page last, I have meandered of and in between the themes of philosophy, theology, psychology, schizophrenia, and of the vernacular with a countenance towards fresh takes and tagalong ideas of a consumptive pragmatism. And by conclusion and page last, I hope my dear reader finds status abound by hope and optimism and perhaps even with a trace of your own personal inspiration. We all must know the night, for this is parcel to our existential plight. But fear of no darkness my dear reader, for if you fixedly gaze to your north there is always a light to illume of your troubles. And I assure, by course of a regular and steady hope-step, safe destiny can always be found and with it follows its companioned correlates of a resolute sense of peace entangled with an undeniable recognizance of the life sublime.

My dear reader:

I have included an adjunct glossary of terms to the text of *On Conquering Schizophrenia* for the purpose of clarity. The terms in this glossary are self-defined and are not verbatim from the dictionary or from other sources. As such, the definitions portray **my** intended meaning as parlance to **your understanding.** I hope you find your glossary experience assistive. Please imbibe and digest as needed!

The bolded words in the text can be found in alphabetical order in the glossary. For ease of read, I bolded the glossary items only upon initial text occurrence rather than every time present.

Prologue

My dear reader, as we begin our literary journey, it is primarily essential to briefly expound in prologue. I must firstly convey some personal items as a reconciliation to our impending communion. *On Conquering Schizophrenia* is my first literary publishing, and its premise rests in the defeat of psychological pathology. I have both lived experience with paranoid schizophrenia, along with extensive professional experience as a mental health therapist. I have been a therapist for over a decade and have been involved in the field of mental health for close to a score. Per a personal choosing, it has always been my preference not to disclose my schizophrenia to others, including coworkers, cohorts, and those whom I am privileged to counsel. I obliquely prefer the meritorious rather the sympathetic.

In *On Conquering Schizophrenia*, I use my personal experience along with my acquisitive clinical acumen to convey the lived experience of schizophrenia and how such personal experiences translate into the clinical perspective including verbiage, terminology, and psychological conceptualization. This perspective is a bridge between those afflicted and those whom treat, and is revelatory to both sides of the treatment paradigm. But the topical content is not meant to be specified for only those with mental health conditions, but rather is intended as a symbolic analogy to the generalized human condition. It is intended for the hands of all who suffer regardless of specificity. Themes of affliction, education, perseverance, humor, faith, and resilience are developed over the course of the narrative and are universal to all as situated in the human condition. *On Conquering Schizophrenia* provides an essential education not only on what can be a most harrowing disease but also to all whom endure affliction. And although I amply share regarding my personal experiences, *On Conquering Schizophrenia* is not implied simply as a personal memoir. Along my proffered course, I also explore numerable canons, including delvings in metaphysics, philosophy, theology, and even the arcane creative process. In bandying among and across diverse literary genres, a broader cognitive perspective is cast and an incremental holistic perspective is satisfied.

It has long been my contention that primarily through education those with schizophrenia and other afflictive promulgations can move beyond precedent limitations, whether derivative of self-imposition or of specified dogmatic "knowledge." For it has been by course of a temporal personal trial that I have come to recognize that palliation universally dwells in pertinent information, quality education, and ultimately in one's own acquisitive wisdom. And once wise to one's affliction, a splendid sort of insight emerges, and one approaches actualization. This is the latent value of sufferance.

I have a master's degree in social work and am currently practicing as a licensed clinical social worker (LCSW). I use compassion, empathy, understanding, and humor as integral availabilities to my treatment protocols and as reliable ethereal and spiritual salves of remediation. I believe it is the combination of astute clinical acumen, along with an authentic human connection, that often heals and consoles. I have a glint in my eye for completion of a second book perhaps on the topic of the misnomers of modern psychology. Such content would once again be a pointed effort to help others in their time of need.

And before we together leap into the literary content just ahead, my dear reader, I offer an ultimate item for your consideration. I propose my writing style to be characteristically two-fold. Firstly, I carry no dispositional pretension. And secondly, I offer no patronization and I rightly assume both your beautiful intelligence along with your inherent merit. And with these given inherent conditions, my dear reader, we proceed together in our literary communion unfettered, undeterred, and with an illumined optimism parceled by a denominated literary favor.

Contents

Chapter 1	Life Begins as Paradoxical Riddle	1
Chapter 2	The Problems of Life are Contained in the Space between People	5
Chapter 3	Enter God	9
Chapter 4	On Tacit Agreement and Social Construct	14
Chapter 5	The Philosophy of Personal Experience	18
Chapter 6	Getting Psychological	22
Chapter 7	Conquering Schizophrenia	30
Chapter 8	Paranoid Schizophrenia	34
Chapter 9	Is a Madman a Safe Man?	54
Chapter 10	Despite Psychosis, the Sun Rises Yet Again	63
Chapter 11	My Most Excellent Elixir!	74
Chapter 12	Away from the Problem and Towards the Solution	79
Chapter 13	Psychological Assimilation	86
Chapter 14	Divine Intervention	92
Chapter 15	Uhh...Hello God?!	99
Chapter 16	In Search of Reality	105
Chapter 17	The Sacred and The Profane	111
Chapter 18	The Sacred Ideal	116
Chapter 19	"I Conclude, God"	119
Chapter 20	Yet Rational Recourse for the Existence of God	123
Chapter 21	Living the Leap	129

1

Life Begins as Paradoxical Riddle

My dear reader, I welcome you to this volume and hope for you interest and joy in your read. As a general overview, for those most interested in the topic of **schizophrenia**, such specified content begins at chapter six. The groundwork to its topic is laid prior. And so together we begin our literary journey in a bounding and mutual lockstep.

 Why write? What is the point? Why create? Is it for myself or is it for others? It is boastful to write for others, I think. It is a seemingly vacuous activity to write for oneself. Nevertheless, there is something urging me to write. It is as almost that I feel compelled. I have never been personally familiar with inspiration but perhaps it is inspiration indeed that is the wellspring of this compulsory feeling to finally put pen to paper.

 Most nonfiction writing is highly logical. It routinely follows in form of premise, body, and derivative conclusion. I too will primarily follow in this manner, although I must forewarn, I am custom to occasional writing tangents. I have learned over the course of many years that pivotal tangents away from topic can be highly therapeutic and a much-needed recourse from taking things all too seriously, especially when the content is of somber theme, much like that of schizophrenia. I also want to establish that what follows is not solely a memoir. At all times, I try and maintain a sense of personal humility and if I think of this writing in the genre of informative memoir it will pain my abdomen with stabs of narcissism. This is why I am hesitant to write. So, this is not an autobiographical memoir. What follows is largely derivative of an intellectual occupation that treks and bandies around the central theme of schizophrenia. Along the way, I also engage in philosophy, dabble in theology, and also try to provide some interjects of humor.

Secondary to the disease of schizophrenia, the contents of my mind have routinely been causal to intensely absurd and utterly confounding experiences with unfathomable existential predicaments and potential ramifications. Enduring chronic, persistently intense, and powerfully adverse experiences with little relent requires a certain type of mindset along with an acquired behavioral methodology. Schizophrenia is a serious topic but make no mistake I would have never survived the disease without using my sense of humor as a coping means to such experienced existential insanities. Good humor is protective. Good humor is adaptive. Good humor is parcel to the cognitive primary that translates to my learned behavioral methodology minor.

So, life begins, and it does so with an abrupt and imposed paradoxical riddle. This riddle can be best understood through the awareness of one's presenting **existential fixations**. Briefly put, existential fixations are the conditions and traits born unto each; and each will have multitudes of such conditions and traits to whom are ascribed. For example, one may be born African-American, in the country of England, to wealthy parents, with no siblings, in a rural setting, and of Catholic faith. Such attributable characteristics are "fixations" because they are existentially imposed and as such are void of any personal choice or rendering. Here is another existentially imposed hypothetical. One may be born in New York City to a drug-addicted mother whom garnered pregnancy through prostitution. Additionally, this newborn arrives of mixed race, with no identifiable father, with a profound intellectual disability, and underdeveloped organicity. There are multitudes of identifiable fixations and the variable combinations of such must approach infinite. Sometimes existential fixations can superficially present as advantageous and other times ostensibly adverse. In my mind, existential fixations could be an important canon of study with potential to the field of behavioral and environmental psychology. The combination of specific fixation sets could not only be explanatory of human behavior but also algorithmically and probability-based predictive.

Existential fixations are intriguing. They are illustrative of that fact that we are born unto an unchosen (and unrequested) **gestalt**. Such traits as race, place or locale of origin, acquired sexual and gender orientations, differentiated spiritual inclinations, financial class distinctions, generalized health, generalized intellect or intelligence, DNA acquisition, inherent personality characteristics, and family system of origin characteristics (including qualitative aspects such as dispositional nurture versus neglect tendencies) are all existentially imposed at birth. Some fixations are easily recognized. Contrarily, others are embedded and are not readily observable. But make no mistake, upon our heralded entrance into this garden of humanity, each of us are assigned our particular combination of fixations. And from a logical perspective, this is a statement of fact beyond single exception and as such is a universal assertion. And certainly the specified fixations I provided is not nearly an exhaustive compilation. Existential fixations are remarkable to consider. Acknowledging the presence of fixations ably mitigates, although certainly does not obliterate, stated assertions and presumptions regarding human "free will." The pop psychology adage is that life is ten percent imposed and ninety percent attitude. To this student of psychology, it is much the reverse. Some ninety percent of life is dictated by fixation and the leftover is attributable to the oft-touted variables regarding good attitude and wise choice. I will not wait for the day when a pop psychologist or motivational speaker addresses a profoundly intellectually disabled, non-ambulatory orphan in the manner of a pep talk regarding the necessity of a good attitude. Rather, I think the teacher in this scenario would be the afflicted and not the proud. To this particular unenlightened mind, life is primarily imposed. Sometimes advantageously, sometimes ferociously, and sometimes of a more neutral manner. Nevertheless, we must proceed with the dictate called life. And we all must do so with what is given.

My hypothesis therefore weighs heavily towards the predominance of existential fixations. Recognizing the consequences and ramifications of existential fixations is highly correlated to a well-developed, deeply embedded sense of empathy for our brethren. Understanding fixations as primary is crucial to understanding humankind's embedded and imposed existential quandaries, afflictions, and specified gestalts. But beyond the givens of imposed existential fixations, what are the variable remains?

Beyond imposed existential fixations enters the dance we call life. And within this do-si-do humankind proceeds with glorified illuminations regarding the **concept** or idea of inherent free will. Contained within this assertion of free will are the remains beyond one's presenting existential fixations. And it is from this launching point, my dear reader, that we begin our literary journey. It is wise to both be aware of what is given unto each as well as cognizance of the proportion left to us through free will. The two dance together throughout this promenade we call life.

In a general manner, therefore, what canons and institutions are prominent in the shaping and developing of the variables contained within the idealized concept of humankind's presenting free will? Canons such as self-help, new age Christianity, and the business of enhancing one's success all dip their toes in the water as specified examples of canons or institutions offering ideals and principles to the individual's exercise of free will. The canons of medicine are participatory and advise us to use our free will to exercise, eat right, and quit smoking. Psychology, technology, economics, philosophy, politics, religion, entertainment, the arts, and charitable programs also play the part in providing potential structure for the execution of one's free will.

Beyond existential fixation belies free will and the two combine in an infinitude of presentations and permutations to form the product we reference as life. This life product becomes the activity over which we scurry. And how do I feel about such scurried activity? Well, in a most pointed manner, I find it highly routine and habituated. Day upon day, I am up at seven, at work by eight, back home by five after a days' work, followed by fine dining (usually pancakes), a little TV, and then off to bed to get up at seven and to do it all once again. I then wash, rinse, dry, and repeat again and again and again. Sound familiar at all? Routine, routine, and more routine. Interestingly, the facts indicate criminals often with the least tolerance for routine. I envy the attitude but not the actions and certainly not the consequences. When I think of routine, I think about **Sisyphus** (of Greek mythology) rolling the rock up and down the hill for all eternity. **Camus** (the philosopher) posited that Sisyphus was happy, but I'm not so certain. I do not like the dailiness of life. At forty-seven years old, I've experienced all that I feel is necessary. There is nothing left that ignites me. I don't even care to be happy. I have dallied with happy and it is not all that impressive. I really question what is left after all these years. Perhaps buying that sports car or perhaps joining the local country club, or better yet, maybe Paris in the spring, or just maybe through hard work and diligence obtaining that big promotion. Really, what is left? I don't even envy the most interesting man in the world. His activities bore me, and I just think he's trying too hard. For what is the empty goal to stress about? To an extent, life is ridiculous. Yes, absurd- I will use the existential term. It can be repetitive, boring, meaningless, pointless, seemingly without end, of void and nothingness, frequently stripped of verified meaning, and just one big unwanted and unrequested inane responsibility. At least, that is what my pessimistic self often thinks. Or, put in another and more simplified manner, as well stated by the great BB King, "the thrill is gone!"

2

The Problems of Life are Contained in the Space between People

Some consider suicide. It is estimated that some forty percent of the population will experience suicidal thoughts at some time over the course of their lives and I believe this to be a conservative underestimation. Having suicidal thoughts is normative. Acting on those thoughts is not. We can all freely contemplate items of our choosing, including without inherent consequence. Thoughts are benign. Actions, however, carry consequence. Common sense dictates that those whom attempt or complete suicide are severely depressed. But more than any other variable, chronic hopelessness is the motor of suicidality. I understand hopelessness. I go through periods of hopelessness. The defining characteristic of hopelessness is feeling relegated to a fixed immutable reality absent of perceived opportunity for positive change, i.e., trapped and ensnared in a dark, damned, and disturbing inalterable state of being. In a vernacular manner, it may be expressed by such phrases as "I am this, or that, and it will always be that way; it will never change." Hopelessness is a deeply profound emotion and can insidiously seethe deep in one's mind, gut, and heart. Hopelessness is a black abyss from whence no change is perceived possible. But there is a glaring caveat that accompanies hope, for its etiology resides in the cognitive. And as such, by its inherent nature, hope is attitudinal in its presentation. Therefore, hope presents as an essential ingredient to the human condition beyond the constraints of existential fixation. Or, in other words, hope is graciously amenable to the efforts of a personal psychological manipulation. And when once amply sourced, hope has the intrinsic quality of garnering an experiential transcendence.

To me, suicidality is understandable. All things considered, I suppose, it can seem like a pretty decent solution to an imposed existential human condition especially given certain existential fixations and certain presenting gestalts. The massive obstacle to suicidal acts is inhibition. I think most humans are born with an innate inhibition that makes it difficult to harm oneself or to annihilate oneself. After all, how does one consciously annihilate oneself without overcoming an innate inhibition? On second thought, however, many humans do commit suicide. Millions. How is this possible? Do similar humans have varying degrees of inhibition? How are some able to overcome inhibition and others cannot? What exactly is the nature of this inhibition? My thinking is there must be an ease for some where there is no ease for others. So, what is the content of this inhibition? I think a few variables may be in play.

Firstly, an inhibition not to destroy oneself is not easily overcome. Secondly, the God card, or belief in God, is preservative. Thirdly, sustenance for the sake of others, i.e., family and friends. And lastly, hope. All these preserve humankind, but not for all. Some overcome inhibitions. Others perhaps may be absent of inhibitions, or at least in such a fervent manner. Some use drugs as a lubricant. Other than that, how do others annihilate or destroy? How does one make ruins of a personal and intimate consciousness? Are some free of these inhibitions altogether? And if they are liberated from preservative inhibitions, is it morally right to commit this most monumental and final act? Is there a moral imperative that also acts as an inhibition? And if one is free from all inhibitions what is to be made of such a choice? We try to prevent suicide because we, as a collective, have values contrary to such an annihilation. In many cases the prevention of suicide can save individuals from impulsive and irreversible acts. Oftentimes, suicide is impulsive and based on perceptions and cognitions that may be distorted and thus correctable. Such an individual can be saved and go on to live a productive and perhaps gratifying life. But what is one to make of those without inhibitions, without any moral imperative, those whom suicide but not of an impulsive act? Rather, a well-planned and contemplated act. Why is society so fervently inclined to judge suicide as necessarily atrocious? Of this I am not so entirely sure, but I can certainly argue a prevailing sense of a projected terse moral judgment. We apparently know better than the uninhibited planner of suicide whom has no moral imperative. This is why suicide is confusing to me.

Returning to the premise, what is one to do therefore with the aspects of life that belie beyond given existential fixation? If one concedes that suicide is not the answer, then what follows? What does one do with this crazy concept called life? This is the $64 million question. The proverbial elephant in the room. It is the question of personal intent. What does one do with the portion of existence not sternly dictated and imposed by existential fixation. The answer is simply, we scurry. We scurry *Of Mice and Men,* and we scurry like **Lilliputians.** But we not only scurry, we also do so in a highly particularized manner. And this is where it gets fascinating. We all proceed according to the rules of life. The only problem is the rules are unwritten. Until now that is. The secret to life is in the unwritten rules. And the unwritten rules reveal that life is contained "in the space between people."

Undoubtedly, there is a tacitness amongst humanity. An unspoken agreement as to what is acceptable and what is unacceptable towards one another. This is termed as "**tacit agreement.**" Is tacit agreement real? It certainly seems to be for what else truly governs the space between individuals and in between societies. This tacitness is the very weave that holds all things together. Tacitness dictates. It dictates it is okay to behave in this manner but not another. It dictates it is okay to say this but not that. But by its inherent nature, tacitness must be recognized by its nebulosity. It resides and exerts beyond a prevailing sense of lawfulness. It is an implied social contract without spoken word or written note. Most are naturally inclined to its parameters. But others, so-called **sociopaths**, violate this relational code and thus are labeled as miscreants. But from where does this tacitness emanate? Is it God or DNA or both? And when did it begin? And how did it evolve? Certainly, at one time, the tacit agreement on slavery, for example, held water but the tacitness evolved, and rightfully so, and transformed. It is truly remarkable that two individuals can look at each other in the eyes and have a basic understanding of what to expect from one another. Oftentimes, the tacitness gets bruised and conflict emerges. Enter divorce or wars. But if the tacit agreement is followed, harmony often occurs, at least for the most part. But from where does it come and without it what becomes of civilization? The complete breakdown of tacit agreement eventually would lead to anarchy, chaos, and social isolation. Individuals would not have groups of belonging. It would be a scary existence.

It is essential to understand that as we scurry about as humans, we do so on the bedrock of tacit agreement. And without the bedrock of tacit agreement, civilization and civility would go the way of extinction. Additionally, and perhaps most importantly, the recognition and affirmative acknowledgment of tacit agreement opens the door for God to enter. Humanity unequivocally depends on tacit agreement. It has not only been sustained but it flourishes in vogue. In the least, tacit agreement is certainly worthy of inclusion in Plato's conception of the ideals. But does it even exceed **Plato's ideals** and reach possible Divine etiology? Has God provided humankind with rules to the game without undue extrapolation and with wise and required subtlety? Is tacit agreement covert evidence of God's existence? Or perhaps is it yet that God is still reeling from Mr. **Nietzsche's** daring and enduring proclamation of "God is dead!"

3

Enter God

What is the primary question most all have about God? In my mind, it has to be the question of existence. If you are philosophical, you are aware of the concept of existence, in and of itself, as a primary and beguiling query. Most all philosophy starts with the question of existence. Without discernments regarding existence primary any following logic is lost. Without knowledge of existence, or nonexistence, all else logically has no foundation. So, philosophy begins with existence primary followed secondarily by assertions regarding knowledge. The philosophical canon regarding the study of existence is known as "**ontology**," and the canon to the study of knowledge is known as "**epistemology**" (the final canon to philosophy is that of "ethics"). But make no mistake, over the course of humanity, existence has been a most beguiling issue for all serious philosophers.

Philosophically speaking, human existence has never been established as a definitive epistemology. One may accept **prima facie** that humanity is alive and well, but this is not coherent theory establishing factual knowledge beyond any doubt. It may feel like splitting hairs, but it is a significant discernment with significant consequences. Many offer theories regarding human existence but no such theory has been established as unquestioned and as a consensus epistemology. And if humans struggle with proof about their own existence, one may well imagine the tumult in trying to establish God's existence. And when reaching this point in epistemological quandary, I always here think of **Einstein**.

Einstein often declared his primary concern was to know the mind of God. I wager that this desire in part may have driven his mathematical and metaphysical ambitions. Ironically, Einstein did not seem concerned with God's existence but rather was more interested in knowing His mind. Einstein was presumptive of God's existence. Personally, I am more preoccupied with God's existence rather than God's mind as without the former the latter is nonsense. But my gut tells me that in his pure genius Einstein may have conceptually known what otherwise eludes the less gifted masses, author included.

The issues of existence and knowledge have plagued philosophers since the dawn of reasoned contemplations. And the existence of self and the existence of God continue to be primary philosophical queries with no apparent proximity to solution. But here my concern is that of God. And the question becomes, do I think God exists? Certainly there is no evidence that has definitively proved the existence of God. All that remains is conjecture and personal opinion, both falling well short of any scientific proof. And to break the bad news, I do not think I am the one to offer any such proof. All I have is my personal experiential evidence. Unfortunately, this does not go all too far when considering matters from a logical perspective. It simply qualifies as a singular testimony and it leaves any generalized conclusions to the intellects of those discerning.

In pertinence to the queries of personal existence and of God's existence, I offer my following testimonies. Firstly, how do I know I exist? Well, generally speaking, I have no definitive evidence or proof. Sometimes it feels like I flicker in and out of existence like the fragile filament in a lightbulb. But mostly, I do think I exist, although I can also look at the world void of my existence. Namely, sometimes I view the world as if I was not present. I sometimes look at humanity and all its drama and activity as if I was not present. Perhaps this is just an idea present to my mind and nothing more. But nevertheless, I think it does raise enough doubt concerning my own existence. And thanks to the genius of René **Descartes**, I have the intellectual faculties to doubt all. All of creation, and everything that is, becomes subject to a series of doubts leading to more doubt and to more doubt. And for clarification, what do I mean by this theoretical doubting exercise? It means doubting layer after layer of all that is, inclusive to such variables as self, mind, perceptions, others, thoughts, work, industry, politics, country, borderlines, social constructs, and very importantly also tacit agreements. And where does this leave the question of personal existence amidst all this doubt? Again, I thank you Descartes for this form of **extreme skepticism**. If all is dubious, all is dubious, and we arrive at a logical tautology. This is the current state of affairs in philosophy.

But beyond tautology, what is left as the remains? I posit only personal experience. It is quite difficult to doubt one's personal experience because it certainly feels real. And the very things I can doubt, I can also experience while doubting. For me, the ground of all is experiential. Beyond extreme skepticism, I believe that which remains is perceived experience. Such personal experience is daily and is well-conditioned. It is chronological by specious second, by minute, by hour. It is vividly contained within the boundaries of the human skin. David **Hume** posited that "**perception is reality.**" Personally, I think more accurately, experience is reality, but I think it would be foolish of myself to project this foundational conjecture on to the lives of others. After all, reality is only my experience. Others may have different ideas. Also, I have great disdain for the term "reality." For after all, how does one describe reality using the term reality? It begs the question. Surer yet then, experience is only my experience. The conclusions from my experience cannot be necessarily projected onto the experiences of others. But, pragmatically speaking, I am comfortable enough with this as my starting point. Perhaps others will have similar experiences and therefore similar conclusions.

Based on my personal experience, I return to the question of does God exist? To answer this question coherently, I must first answer "what is God?" If one asks, "what is God," one will necessarily begin to use human concepts to describe the qualities of God. To me, that is unsatisfactory. God is transcendent of human attributions. So where does one go to get out of this paradoxical situation? In lieu of this conundrum, I return to my foundational grounding, that being, personal experience. So, what does my personal experience indicate regarding this matter of the attributes of God? The question of God is a dogged and persistent question in my experience. And again, any descriptors and/or concepts I attribute to God are based on my singular experience. This being the case, I cannot infer any of my personal findings to be logically generalizable. But nevertheless, for the moment this must suffice, and together we persist.

The Godhead of Judaism, Catholicism, ancient Greece, Pentecostal, Mormon, Methodist, and Agnostic all have their version of God and Deity. Add to this nary of a list atheistic and humanistic narratives and the doubts are cast regarding the issue of Divine existence. But I am not writing for the purposes of persuasion. Rather, only for purposes of navigating my own personal experiences. If others can relate, all the better. If not, let it be discernment. Are their many Gods or only one God? Certainly, the existence of only one God makes comprehension of all things easier but perhaps not more accurate. Humans under one God with like others is easily comprehended, but in my experience simply not the sole possibility. If the conceptual framework of all under one God was thoroughly persuasive and vivid to my mind, this thing I call personal experience would be much easier to discern. Unfortunately, this is not the case. It's all much more dynamic and shifting than this singular notion. I wish it were not the case, but experientially it is. And from this confusing state of affairs the wise adage of "beware all ye who enter here" enters my mind heeding me to only proceed further with much due caution for possible treachery awaits.

I suppose there's a certain logic to it all. A muddled logic but nevertheless some organizing principles. The organizing principles again revolve around personal experience; after all, experience is the bedrock and foundation to my philosophy. It may not be a secure bedrock, loose rocks and all, but a bedrock nonetheless. So based on my experience, what qualities do I project onto my personal Deity?

Firstly, and I think quite interestingly, I project God as male. In general, gender identity is often attributed to God and is often assumed without much consideration. I find this gender identity attribution peculiar, in a sense, because God is transcendent and therefore why not gender transcendent? Next, I also project having one God for myself. The reason I feel there is a personal God and creator, in part, is I cannot fathom myself as the creator of myself. If I created myself, I would be the creator. But my experience, as for now, tells me I am not my own creator. Hence, the creator of myself exists. Perhaps more succinctly it could be said, I have a personal creator or perhaps even creators. I am a singular entity, created by another differentiated creator or even perhaps multiple differentiated creators. But, in general, for whatever reason, I feel most comfortable with a singular God as my creator.

In the overarching and general conceptualizations of modern Deity, I find the Eastern versus Western views of deity interesting in their dichotomies. In the West, God is often described by his presence. In the East, God is often described by his absence. It is an interesting contrast from West to East, that being presence versus absence. Presence I think is easily understood, at least superficially. Comprehending absence may prove to Westerners a bit more strenuous but that is simply due to the varying cultural contexts. In the East, God's absence is also frequently referred to as "emptiness" or "nothingness." Superficially, from West to East, God is perceived in contrarian manners. But although these are dichotomous perspectives, I do not find them as necessarily irreconcilable perspectives. When viewed on a spectrum, I find these contrarian views as reconcilable and plausibly indicative of the same singular God or Deity.

In my experience, the concept of God becomes confusing primarily due to the existence of other people. After all, I have no idea if the others I perceive are in fact people, the same species, or being that I consider myself. For me to vividly believe that others are the same as I, I would have to have experience of being other and that has yet to happen. More pointedly, I would have to steadfastly believe in social constructs. In my experience, social constructs are not rigid and steadfast but rather are loosely existent. In the absence of a strong belief regarding social constructs, there is no personal experience of other and therefore I am back to my bedrock of a singular personal experience and its correlated evidence.

The idea of a social construct is similar to the idea of tacit agreement. Both have to do with the space between people. In the space between people there are gaps and voids. These gaps and voids are filled by both social constructs and tacit agreements. Without humanistic belief in the phenomena of tacit agreement and social construct, variables I refer to as the space between people, our sense of reality would be thrown into flux and chaos. Tacit agreement and social constructs are two prominent ideas that contribute to our sense of a shared reality. There does seem to be a code, an ethic, and an understanding between members of this world. I wonder from whence this code comes? Is it of innate genome or is it of divine origination? An interesting query, no doubt. It is another existential problem for which I do not definitively know the answer. This code allows for civilization, but civilization is not necessarily a predetermined and necessary value in and of itself. Perhaps the code is found in the Divine. Perhaps just in humanity. So, which of the two is it? Please allow me to explore.

4

On Tacit Agreement and Social Construct

If there is an existing divinity, an ordained interjection of tacit agreement and social construct into the space between people is highly sensible at least to this particular perceiving mind. But **metaphysics** coupled with explanatory ease is a rare combination. Potential problems and alternate possibilities always emerge to posited metaphysical theories. Pertaining to the divine, consider for example the inherent conceptual dichotomies between monotheistic and polytheistic world views. I harken back to the days of the Greeks who were polytheistic. Greek theology posited numerous existing Gods with varying particularized characteristics and purposes. The Gods interacted with one another and were embedded in a sort of hierarchy of divinity with the god Zeus as a Godhead. In more recent times, monotheism seems to have gained much momentum. For example, the Catholics, Jews, and Muslims all point to a singular Deity. But, of course, as with all things there are complications. Take for example the Catholic faith. The Catholic faith proliferates the Godhead into the Father, Son, and Holy Spirit. The faith also has numerous additional spiritual figures of high regard including troops of saints, angels, apostles, and disciples. A little bit of something for everyone, I suppose. I now ask, is this a monotheistic orientation or something otherwise? All this leads me to the conclusion that to posit tacit agreement and social construct as divinely derivative again begs the question. It begs the question of God's existence in the primary. In this man's opinion, this muddies the water plenty enough to throw the origin of tacit agreement and social construct again into an unknown abyss.

Perhaps the concepts of tacit agreement and social construct are of humanistic design and origin. Namely, if the Godhead is eliminated, is tacit agreement and social construction the doing of a humanistic effort and creation? And if so, how did it originate and due to what need or cause? Namely, are the concepts of tacit agreement and social construct inherently part if the human genome or alternatively were they perhaps derivative of a deliberate human undertaking in furtherance of specified values such as quality and quantity of life. Firstly, however, it should be noted that even if tacit agreement and social constructs are of humanistic origin, it also undoubtedly has to be admitted that they often are violated and violated harshly. Murder, robbery, rape, betrayal, abuse, criminality, fraud, assault, and malevolent social exchanges, amongst others of multitudes, are all examples of broken tacit agreements and broken social constructs. And, as we all well know, these violations of the moral codes are all too frequent. Just look to the daily headlines. Nonetheless, the unwritten codes of tacit agreement and social construct do persist in human society, at least for the large part, and they play a vital role in human relationships and society. I certainly cannot go back in time to identify the seemingly nebulous etiology and time of initiation of these codes. All I am aware of is being born and conditioned into these implicit codes. And for a time in my life, these unwritten codes were both gladly accepted and most assured. But, as I age, the less I know. And the less I know, the more I doubt the existence of any tried and true code. Therefore, if these concepts are humanistic in origin, this too has now become dubious to my mind. And I think it must be well conceded that any such codes are frequently violated. And due to these frequent violations, it leads me to wonder if these codes really exist at all. Perhaps tacit agreement and social construct are just products of my imagination. Perhaps they are simply bogus. Or perhaps, alternatively and more optimistically, they are in fact real and are in vogue. Perhaps my doubt is simply cast due to outlier violations. And thus, I have arrived once again at an ambiguous and most unsatisfying conclusion. And when confronted with such conclusive ambiguities, I tend to return to philosophy. Philosophy always directs me to the essential fundamentals of given issues and is a useful practice to understanding issues in a most logical, orderly, and coherent manner. But make no mistake, philosophy is no panacea. It too presents with inherent self-imposed limitations that always mitigates any posited epistemological certainties.

I have always used the term philosophy as a similitude of returning to the very basics and foundations of argumentation. But is philosophy itself merely an intellectual exercise and void of any real fruit? Well, let's take a look. Firstly, it has to be said there have been some great minds who have written a few lines in the field of philosophy. I have read many of the great philosophers and admittedly many a time the terminology is confusing (for a variety of reasons), and therefore the arguments are difficult to most accurately discern. I cannot always definitively and cogently follow philosophical argumentation. But at other times, I can, and I get the gist of things. And as a fun tangent of sorts, in my estimation here are some of the greatest philosophers of the ages: Socrates, Plato, **Aristotle** (a.k.a., the great organizer; I love his tagline), Seneca, St. Thomas Aquinas, David Hume, Renée Descartes, Michele Foucault, Jacques Derrida, Bertrand Russell, Soren **Kierkegaard**, Fyodor Dostoevsky, Jean-Paul Sartre, Friedrich Nietzsche, Ayn Rand, Viktor **Frankl**, Martin Heidegger, Ken Wilber, Karl Marx, Carl Yung, Albert Einstein, the giant Immanuel Kant, Marshall McLuhan, and Gregory Bateson, among many others. I hold affinity for Derrida, Dostoevsky, and Bateson and my general inclination leans towards existentialism. Many cords of pages have been written among these philosophers, yet no undisputed epistemology has yet been achieved. Philosophers are classically known to gladly obliterate the previous philosopher's theory. And to date, philosophers have been successful in mitigating even the greatest of philosophical theories, and as such it leaves absolutely no posited philosophical theory by any philosopher of any age void of dubiousness. This is to say at least to this current time in history. The great David Hume would argue, however, that an infinitude of cause A with effect B in the past does not necessarily mean a cause and effect in the present or for the future. Nevertheless, to date, all philosophical and metaphysical theories have in fact been critically mitigated, if not whole-handedly scrapped, altogether. What remains are simply unproven hypothesis and theories. Some may be more persuasive than others and some may be tantalizing depending on personal inclination. Nevertheless, there has been no single posited philosophical theory that has stood absent of warranted logical criticisms. Once a deficiency in a theory is discovered, then the pig-pile really ensues. And as pertaining to tacit agreement and social construction, I apprehend in a logical manner that what remains is simply my theory. And in part, this is the function of philosophy altogether. Philosophy is nothing more than learning to formulate your own theories regarding life. Philosophy is often misunderstood. Its intent is not dogmatic theory. Its intent is to provide one the intellectual courage to formulate and assert personal perspective and opinion. Once it is understood that one's personal opinions will always be subject to opposing perspectives and criticisms, then the work of philosophy is done. What remains is personal belief not to be swayed by the masses. And when of firm belief, and beyond the whims of the many, that which can emerge is not only personal belief but also personal conviction. And personal conviction can be transformative both to the self and to the whole of mankind. Only open any history book and in its pages will be found profound figures of firm conviction. A man once said, "**I have a dream**!" I love that personal conviction! What a courageous man!

5

The Philosophy of Personal Experience

Amidst much skepticism and dubiousness, I persist undeterred and I return to my personal theory and my personal foundation- that being, the idea of personal experience. Philosophical theory often begins with an assertion of self-evidence. Self-evidence is the genesis from which further argumentation occurs, or in other words, there needs to be a starting point and the best starting points begin with self-evidence. Self-evidence is that which is logically tautological and therefore beyond the need of further proof. Tautological self-evident premises are the gold standard on which coherent theories are constructed. If one does not concur with the primary self-evident premise, then any derivative theory can been quickly disregarded. If one agrees with the posited self-evident premise, then further exploration may be warranted. I consider my personal experience to be self-evident and as thus is beyond the need of further proof. My personal experience is the self-evident genesis and premise from which I base my derivative conclusions. And this leads me in a new direction, at this point. Based on my personal experience, that which I find self-evident, what derivatives do I find most pertinent to ably getting along in this thing we call life?

All I have direct access to is my personal experience and nothing beyond. I do not have direct access to the experience of others. Therefore, by manner of a judicious logic, my conclusions are solely derivative of my personal experience. I find my personal experience to be my genesis. It is my tautological first premise and as such belies beyond the need of any further evidentiary proof. Either others acquiesce to the premise or they do not. And by the means of a maturing intellect, I have concluded that any "knowledge" from others turns out to be, at best, solely a source of friendly advice regarding its correlated topical. Knowledge from others does not derivatively equate to knowledge for oneself. And again, by knowledge, I am referring to what is best known and least subject to dubiousness and fervent skepticism. Many centuries of effort have been fruitless in pursuit of confirmed metaphysical knowledge with no current prevailing consensus. Rotund theories become routinely obliterated by the next deep thinker. So how does one go about retrieving answers to important questions without any preordained knowledge? Perhaps knowledge will never be found and perhaps knowledge will never be universal. And perhaps trying to find generalizable "knowledge," that is, "knowledge" that is both true for you, me, and for all others, across all cultures and chronology, is a misguided pursuit altogether. Perhaps there is no such knowledge. For thus far, across millennials, this has been the case. A knowledge that is true for you and me, and all others, has proven futile. But why is this so?

Well firstly, let us not to reinvent the wheel. There is a difference between pragmatic knowledge and metaphysical knowledge. Pragmatic knowledge is in no short supply while metaphysical knowledge is nil in supply. What is pragmatic knowledge? Pragmatic knowledge gets us through the day. Pragmatic knowledge is highly utilitarian. Pragmatic knowledge consists of the things we know to be true in different fields of study. There are highly utilitarian knowledge bases in such fields as, but certainly not limited to, automotives, plumbing, computer science, electrical, dietary science, medicine, and homebuilding. Without the fruits of this type of pragmatic knowledge there would be a massive regression in one's personal quality of life and more generally to society as a whole. No doubt, there appears to be a pragmatic knowledge ably functioning within the confines of my personal experience; and perhaps yours as well. Perhaps pragmatic knowledge bridges my world to yours. I just felt compelled to address what others may point to as knowledge. I do not consider pragmatic knowledge the same as metaphysical knowledge. They are **two and not one**. The one is highly practical and the other highly theoretical.

Returning to the very foundation of this written exercise, that being of "my personal experience," allow me to clarify this recurrent textual phrasing by definition and intent of meaning. Once clarified, my personal ontology can then logically follow accompanied by a recognized cogency. I think of personal experience like a sum total. From the first waking blink in the morning to the last of the day, and then whatever happens in the sleeping dream-state. Experience is more than just perception. Perception is limited to the senses. Experience is something a bit richer, I think. Experience includes data collected by the senses, but it does not end there. Experience also includes memory, visualizations, ideas, and beliefs and it is characterized by innumerable variables of content and context. It also includes one's relationships and how those relationships have evolved over time. Experience connects past, present, and future. One's mind threads together all that is into orderly experiences. Experience is an element of consciousness that makes connections from disparate phenomenon. Or, put another way, if I were to ask another to tell me her life story her narrative would be that of her life experience. And yet, even if the life narrative be of brevity or of great length, the narrative itself still would not capture experience in its totality or richness. It would be but an excerpt. Experience too is embedded in time and over time. Experience changes as one develops through the chronological life stages. The experience of a ten-year-old is in no way comparable to the experience of a ninety-year-old other than both being experiential to the particular individual. The content of these varying experiences could not be more disparate, but, nonetheless, they both are inherently grounded by the same item called experience. Experience, therefore, has universality because it is common to all humankind in that we all have experiences. But additionally, experience is also singularly specified because each individual has her own differentiated experiential content. No two humans have identical experiential content over time, but nevertheless do have the commonality of having experience in and of itself. Experience casts a wider net than David Hume's "perception is reality." The sum of experience is greater than perception alone.

When creating a premise, and then followed by a philosophy, the premise is the foundation or the first to all that follows. And characteristically, any such sound premise cannot recede into an **infinite regress**. It must stand alone. In other words, the premise to an argument cannot not rely on prior argument. This would be the logical fallacy of an infinite regress. Therefore, the premise is first and primary and absent of precedence. Ultimately, based on the supporting evidence, one either comes to accept the premise or one arrives at its denial. The most salient premises therefore contain the characteristic of self-evidence. Self-evidence is the starting point for a foundational premise. I hold experience, both in its uniqueness and commonness, as self-evident to all humans. We all have an idea of personal experience without much need for lengthy definition or ornate description. Experience is base and life itself is its correlate. In my thinking, experience is primary and all else is secondary.

From a first premise follows its consequential derivatives. This is the manner by which theories are constructed. If a cogent theory becomes reputable then instigates the process of its analytical dissection. Once critically parsed by others the argument then either becomes discarded in total or perhaps by piecemeal. From this typical refutation the next dance of argumentation then begins. But my point in writing, my dear reader, is not for purposes of philosophical argument. But I did want to provide clarification in regard to how I view premises, argumentation, and types of knowledge. I also wanted to explain my base premise and the importance of first premises in argumentation. Effective first premises always will have a quality of self-evidence. For my purposes, experience is the self-evident concept from which all else is derivative. What follows from here, therefore, are my thoughts and reflections on my personal experience. Along the way, perhaps there will be some experiential similarities between yours and mine and, as such, may follow mutual empathies and an experiential communion. In the descriptions of my experiences, I will move away in part from philosophical overtones and more to matters of a psychological nature including some of the psychology embedded in the totality of my experiences. And I have to wonder if these personal experiences of mine, as I will describe, can be of any help or hope to others.

6

Getting Psychological

Where does one begin in the description of personal experience? In psychology, more specifically **psychotherapy**, there is an approach called **narrative therapy**. Narrative therapy is the method a therapist may use to draw out a client's life story to understand that individual and to reframe parts of the life story to reduce any **dystonic** feelings. But heed not my dear reader, for I have no intention of a personal life narrative. Instead, I would like to focus on certain aspects of my experience that perhaps are the most interesting rather than addressing the totality of experience. A complete narrative, therefore, is not what interests me (this would be more autobiographical). Rather, I prefer to just focus on the most intriguing and informing parts of my experience.

I suppose that this is as good of a time as any to touch on the mental illness in my life. At about age twenty-one, soon after completing my undergraduate college studies, a psychotic disorder invaded my mind and eventually I was diagnosed by professionals and doctors with "Schizophrenia, paranoid type." This was the label that was applied to my mind in my early twenties. Professionally, about ten years after my initial diagnosis, in my early thirties, I went back to college and received a master's degree in social work (**MSW**). It has now been over a decade since that graduation and degree. In the meanwhile, from graduation to the current time (2018), I have worked primarily as a therapist in the field of mental health and some in the substance abuse field. My official title and credentials are as a Licensed Clinical Social Worker, and I also have a license to work in schools. So, to best understand my writing on my experiences it is best understood with this gestalt. Namely, I was diagnosed with mental illness in my early twenties, and thereafter graduated with a master's degree in my mid-thirties in social work. Since obtaining the master's degree, I have worked in the fields of social work, mental health, and psychology. All my work as a therapist came after the initial onset of issues with mental illness and psychosis. To fully get the gist of what I am describing, it is best to remember this context. My experiences will be best understood with the paranoid schizophrenia diagnostic in mind alongside my master's education and subsequent professional experience.

I went to undergraduate college and received a B.A. in communications with a minor in philosophy (you would have never guessed about the philosophy, huh?). My undergraduate studies were intended to prepare me for a job in broadcasting (or television production), most likely behind the camera in some capacity. I did pursue this career path after college for a couple of years and even worked at two local television stations for a brief time. I also worked on a film, various TV commercials, and on some very exciting corporate videos (sarcasm intended). During this time, in my early twenties, also came the initial onset of the schizophrenia. Nevertheless, I continued to pursue broadcasting undeterred for a couple more years until a much needed twist of fate (perhaps of divine origin) pointed me in a new direction. This new direction was entirely predicated on the onset of paranoid schizophrenia. Without schizophrenia, social work as a vocation would have never occurred. So, was schizophrenia a blessing or a detriment? To this day, my inclination wavers. Like most things, I suppose, it is likely a combination of sorts. Things in life rarely present as entirely congruent. But just to finish my thoughts on my broadcasting career, it was mainly what I considered physical or manual labor with the added responsibility of learning how to operate various types of machinery, i.e., cameras, lighting, video recording machines, and electrical patchwork. It was not overly intellectual, and my body primarily served the conduit to profitability. Then, in a most unpredictable and amazing manner, fate intervened, and I was off to a new vocational focus. I have absolutely no rational understanding how things changed so drastically in my life and in such an unplanned manner. In no way did I enjoy the career path of working in the media. And if not for the onset of schizophrenia, I would have never transitioned into social work.

My last words on my undergraduate communications degree is that behind the scenes in broadcasting for me was just uninspiring and uninteresting. It did not fit my personality very well. And so, in conjunction with the hands of time, the broadcasting career was set aflame and most thankfully so. In a most remarkable manner, schizophrenia, which is generally considered an unwanted affliction, unequivocally facilitated a much needed and drastic career change to a vocation much better aligned with my interests and aptitudes. All this change and nothing of my own doing. Go figure. I suppose, "the best made plans *Of Mice and Men*."

I will soon return to the topic of schizophrenia and in a most thorough and hopefully illuminating manner. I believe the information I must share may be helpful to others both to those with the diagnostic and also to those who treat them. But before doing so, now given the described background pertaining to the schizophrenia, along with the vocational considerations, I return to my premise. Experience is my foundation. There is nothing baser than my experience. Philosophically, my experience is my first premise. As a first premise, there really is nothing to support it. In other words, it stands alone as a starting point. And as a starting point, it rests on self-evidence. When self-evidence is posited, it is another way to say "first premise without need of further proof." Self-evidence is the first truth to a philosophy and from the first truth all else is derived. Over the course of the history of philosophy, all the great philosophers start with a first premise. As I have previously described, once a philosopher establishes a pertinent first truth or self-evident premise, the next philosopher often will refute the premise and therefore critically minimize the derivative philosophy. This is part of the ebb and flow of philosophical argumentation.

When I was in college, one of my professors (William **Bradford**) who taught epistemology, that being the branch of philosophy regarding "knowledge," introduced the class to his own book. His epistemological philosophy started with a first premise as well. To give you an idea of a first premise from someone other than myself, his first premise proposed a methodology that established the necessary proof of existence. His first premise was that singling out an object with a minimum of two sensory faculties confirmed its existence. In other words, the chair exists because I can "see" it and also "touch" it. The chair was identified by two separate sensory faculties. Of course, this is an ultra-simplistic description of the philosophy, but it is an example of another first premise. From this first premise his philosophy followed.

Perhaps the most famous first premise ever posited was by Renée Descartes. Descartes posited "**I think, I am.**" Descartes systematically doubted all things to find a first premise he could not doubt. He engaged in this methodology to find an absolute certainty and therefore an indubitable epistemology. He concluded "I think, I am." His doubting methodology is legendary amongst philosophers. Ultimately, he concluded, the one thing he could not doubt was that he was a thinking creature. He could not doubt that he had thoughts. This was his foundation to his philosophy. Descartes, therefore, concluded "I think, I am."

This was his first self-evident premise to his philosophy. And just to be clear, no first premise has ever been proved, at least in a metaphysical sense, although by no means does this necessarily negate the idea entirely since we must begin somewhere.

Another legendary first premise is contained in The United States Declaration of Independence. It begins with the first premise of "We hold these truths to be self-evident, that all men are created equal" and have the right to "life, liberty, and the pursuit of happiness." From this first premise, the idea of America was launched. This is a testament to the vital importance of a first premise. Without the idea of self-evident truths the formation of this great country may have never come to be. "All men are created equal" is beyond further proof and is plainly self-evident. The whole idea of equality that we are so familiar with was not always a familiar idea. But the idea of equality is now embedded into the values of the United States. Perhaps the greatest of all ideas in the course of humankind, that being the United States, was conceived based on self-evident premises. It proves the power of a first premise and how a first premise can significantly influence the course and values of humankind. Certainly, my first premise is not going to carry any such weight. Some ideas are brilliant and transformative and the rest fall in line somewhere behind. Nevertheless, I will further explain aspects of my first premise, that being, personal experience.

Experience is personal. It is my own. Experience is intimate. It is part of who I am. The presence of my experience does not necessarily implicate that others also have typical characteristic experience, although I feel it to be likely. Like all first premises, mine too will be susceptible to contrarians. That being the case, I will further explain the term experience and then I will refute it myself and allow the contrarians to rest. Once refuted, I will then return wholeheartedly and with conviction to my first premise. From this self-evident source, my derivatives will follow. And all derivatives, as is true of any theory, will be constituted on an implicit **"leap of faith."** Any such leap is the inferential act one undertakes from first premise to all its subsequent derivatives. The inferential leap is the necessary logic for the continuance of any theory or derivative philosophy.

An important aspect of "personal experience" involves time. I can order my experiences chronologically in my mind. I can remember experiences that occurred twenty years ago versus ones that have happened ten years ago versus the experience I am currently having at this very moment. It should be said that experience does not include future time. I could project what an experience may be like in the future, but it is not yet an experience. The projection of the future, however, does contribute to the unfolding of my present experience. In describing experience in time-related terms, it is noted that all experience occurs in specious time and is etched in the subjective faculty of memory in varying degrees of voracity. Some experiences are vividly etched into the tapestry of memories while others are easily forgotten. Time is embedded in experience.

My experience is highly personal and is mine alone. I cannot simply infer that others have similar experiences as they may be quite disparate. I try to keep this in mind when reflecting about others and their personal experience. My experience is like a container of various concepts. Inclusive to this container is my experience of "thoughts." Of course, the term thoughts is a very common intrapsychic construct used in our shared vernacular reality. In my experience, thoughts present as a psychological chatter of sorts that includes variables such as language, visualizations, words, ideas, personal conversation, and problem-solving. Thoughts serve many functions and often seem to be highly utilitarian. Thoughts get me through the day. They seem to provide directives, but they also can produce confusion and frustration. The presence of thoughts may often be taken for granted as parcel to what it means to be human. Nevertheless, I am continually amazed as to why I have these things called thoughts. I certainly did not choose to have thoughts. For some unknown reason these things we call thoughts seemingly carry eminence to the human experience. Thoughts can be highly variable, contextual, and with emotional overtones. Thoughts can be humorous, frightening, disturbing, sublime, taboo, benign, uninspiring, inspirational, evil, good, banal, repetitive, novel, and curious. They are artifacts to my experience and they are instrumental in many ways to my sustenance.

From whence do thoughts derive? With certainty, I do not know of their origin. This harkens back to Descartes's dogma. Descartes put thoughts as primary to "I am" or to his existence. In other words, because he has thoughts and he then derivatively arrives at his existence. As for myself, I have thoughts, but I do not know of their origin. Specifically, and importantly, I have thoughts that at times seem to arise without any provocation. Other times, my thoughts seem to derive from another aspect of my experience that I label as identity. Sometimes my identity seems to be the origin of my thoughts, or in other words, derivative from Descartes's "I." Other times, however, it is the reverse and thoughts seem to lead to identity. I am not exactly sure which is primary-that being, my thoughts or my identity. They seem to have an interplay amongst one another, each edifying and shaping the other over time. In other words, the "I" producing thoughts, and the thoughts mutually producing the "I." Therefore, part of my experience also involves the concept of identity that is shaped in part by its corresponding and highly habitual thought content.

Inclusive to my sum of experience is the concept of identity. Identity is a centering in the midst of experience but is also variable over time. The identity I had as a ten-year-old versus my current identity is different but it is also integrated. My identity can shift from specious moment to specious moment but paradoxically can also exist as stable over periods of time. It appears to me that as I age, identity has become more variable and less stable. As part of my identity, included is a concept called "name." My name is "Robert" and this name is part of my identity. In my thoughts, I often refer to myself by this name, a so-called "Robert," and it presents as a conglomerated concept. It seems to be integral and inclusive to my identity. Name seems to be a unifying concept to my identity and it often recurs in my thoughts. There are other aspects to identity, as well. How I appear through my sensory data, or how I "look," also contributes to identity. This too is variable. Sometimes I look in a particular fashion and other times another.

Sensory data also contributes to my experience. The things I see, hear, touch, smell, and taste contribute to my conception of experience. I recently heard someone speak of an inherent sixth sense akin to extrasensory perception (ESP) or a form of refined intuition. I like the courage of challenging the norm, but currently I remain well-suited to the five. Sensory data interplays with thoughts and identity contributing to a sum experience. I find it difficult to a identify which is primary as they seem to dance with one another. Sensory data is variable as well. It seems to be consistent over time, although recently, for example, my sight has become variable. It was once very clear and now it is somewhat blurred. Changes in sensory faculties do occur, like diminished eyesight or compromised hearing, and it subsequently can influence aspects of my experience.

Another input variable to my sum experience are my presenting "moods." Moods often reflect how well my generalized experience is proceeding. Moods such as sadness, melancholy, apathy, **euthymia**, anxiety, calmness, confidence, dejection, optimism, and pessimism are all potential moods that can describe how I may feel at any point in time during my temporal experience. Moods can be relatively persistent or more fleeting, but inevitably over time present are variable as well. Favorable moods contribute to more desired experiences and adverse moods to more laborious experiences. Markedly, positive moods, in my experience, are usually fleeting and short in duration. This is just parcel to my experience. Most often, however, my mood is characteristically neutral (clinically known as euthymia). Euthymia is the relative medium on the spectrum of felt emotions and generally is clinically considered a healthy baseline emotional presentation. Interestingly, "happiness" is a mood or state of being that is primarily absent in my life and experience. I do not seek happiness and I rarely think about happiness. It has always been a non-factor in my life. I do not see this as a problem or deficit but just as an experiential **scotoma**. Perhaps this is a good **tao** because, as far as I discern, happiness is more a derivative consequence of noble intent rather than an existing passive precedent neglect of instigation.

Another aspect of my experience is something I call "context." Context seems to embed experience in time. Context is highly variable as well. Context is my current being-in-the-environment and as situated in time and place. Context can be linguistically construed, for example, by such phrases as "in the morning, afternoon, now, last year, when I was ten, tomorrow, and last night" just to name a few. Context also embeds me in the concept of "location." In my experience, I seem to be present in an "environment." In other words, I seem to be at a location or place. For example, I am currently at the library. When I leave I will be outdoors, followed by being in my car, and then at the store. I will then be in the car again and then I will return to the location I refer to as home. Locations have a macro and a micro availability as well. For example, I am currently at the library. If I wanted to look in a more macro perspective, however, I could conceive of being at the library, in my quaint village, in the state of New York, in the country of the United States, situated on the Earth, within the solar system, embedded in the Milky Way galaxy, and present within the vast universe. This exercise too can be executed to a presenting micro perspective. A last note about location, as part of experience, is the very unusual trait of "familiarity." Locations usually seem familiar to my sensory data. Locations resemble each other in many ways although no two such locations are characteristically exact. A most interesting aspect pertaining to location is the feeling of being "lost." Feeling lost indicates a micro disorientation. And although I may feel lost per se, the specific location always resembles other locations characteristically familiar. Additionally, if I visit a foreign location on just a few occasions, it suddenly becomes known and familiar like the rest. Sometimes being in an unfamiliar location can cause the mood of anxiety. But once familiar with the location, a sense of comfort often settles in with its increasing familiarity. A most peculiar aspect to me about location is the uncanny resemblance that all locations have with one another. Additionally, there is also a comfort through exposure. When I see repeated pictures of our blue marble, the Earth, familiarity ensues and I am comforted as to my relative location. At the same time, one must admit the idea of our macro location is somewhat bizarre. And the greater the macro perspective the greater the peculiarity. Another consideration to location is that locales are only known as mediated through my senses. That being the case, I have no certainty if locations intrinsically exist external of their appearances to my senses (a most **solipsistic** thought). Therefore, if I had no senses at all would locations exist at all? Certainly, I find this to be an unanswerable. Nevertheless, regardless of this uncertainty, my experience persists.

Another aspect pertaining to my personal experience is my favored idea of gestalt. Gestalt is an established psychological term referring to the nebulous sum total of personal experience. Gestalt considers all factors to experience and additionally it takes a transcendent intrapsychic and systemic overview of the totality. Gestalt integrates all and provides feedback regarding all things considered. It is a super-macro feedback pertaining to experience. The well-known euphemism of "life is good" is an essential example of a stated gestalt. Gestalt takes all things into account plus one.

There are multitudes of variables in infinite combinations as potential inputs to my experience. As for now, however, the last ingredient to my experience I would like to address is regarding the concept of "control." And more specifically, the question of "am I in control of my experience?" The answer to this loaded question turns out to be both "yes" and "no" along with explicable caveats. If I were in total control of my experience, I suppose I would be perpetually enmeshed in satisfactory experiences. In other words, my experiences would be as I purposefully intended at all times and perpetually satisfying. I would be the dictator to all my experiences and they would be unanimously as I desired. Prima facie, however, this is not the case. Alternatively, I have already posited my thoughts on existential fixation along with the psychological remains of human free will. So in a general sense, the answer is both yes and no. A little of both so to say. But for now, let's leave it simply stated. Any further exploration I most assuredly offer will only lead to an infinite regress. The concept of control makes for a most excellent introductory philosophical lesson. The concept very ably teaches "infinite regress" along with its baffling existential quandaries. But let's not walk that path today because as for now reality beckons.

7

Conquering Schizophrenia

I have described some concepts as they relate to my personal experience. I offer that personal experience is embedded in a larger system otherwise referred to as reality. It is integral to understand that concepts and reality are very much of the same tapestry. Concepts are base and provide meaning to interpersonal relationships and communication. When combinations of concepts are sequenced and shared with one another, they create a social context. This shared social context becomes the constructed reality.

Now with the essential groundwork in place, what follows is the bridgework between the concepts of schizophrenia and reality. And frankly, the correlates and diversions related to these two concepts is the primary tour de force of this endeavor. And this next item of offering is of the highest importance when conquering schizophrenia. Because of its importance, the next five sentences are associated in meaning but alternatively phrased in hope of reaching you, my dear reader, by manner of a mutual clarity.

Schizophrenia is a break from consensus reality.
Schizophrenia is no longer sharing in the consensus reality.
Schizophrenia means one is out of step with the rest of consensus reality.
Schizophrenia is a universe unto itself detached from the rest.
Schizophrenia is understood as a disease pertaining to one who is detached from reality or "out of touch" with reality.

Before conquering schizophrenia, it is vital to understand the relationship of the disease to the concept known as "reality." Understanding this vital relationship is primary to conquering schizophrenia. What follows is my best attempt to detail the schizophrenic experience and how it relates to the greater reality. The information is meant to salvage lives. It is a genuine offering of how to survive and thrive with schizophrenia. The information is intended for both those who have schizophrenia and also for those who clinically treat them. I must forewarn, however, that the offering is not inherently simplistic. I had to address the need for certain parameters before delving into life with schizophrenia. Now that I have established these parameters we move onto conquering schizophrenia.

The attribution of the concept of schizophrenia was applied to my mentality in my early twenties. I am now in my mid-forties and the label to my experience persists. But fear not, my dear reader, for together we persist together with motive to conquer. But prior to kicking schizophrenia ass (humor intended), first allow me to provide some basic information on the umbrella term of "mental illness" under which the specific diagnostic of schizophrenia belies. When I think of the concept of mental illness, its antonym also emerges as a concept to my mind, that being "mental health." The term mental health is more generalized and could be applicable to all in the general population. In other words, all those in the population could answer the query "how is your mental health today?" Contrarily, mental illness is more specific to a subset of the population. After all, it would not be proper to ask the general population "how's your mental illness today?" I think at some point in the future the term mental illness will ultimately become a politically incorrect term. The term indicates **pathology** and deficit and I think a more holistic term is better suited. But as I age, I seem less concerned with the political correctness of a term and more interested in its meaning and content. So you can call it mental illness, pathology, madness, or craziness it really makes no difference to me. I once was sensitive to language but I am no longer. I am more interested in the idea.

What is mental illness? As I previously referenced, mental illness applies to a subset of the population. Within this subset are individuals with varying types of mental illness. This further parses the population into smaller and smaller subsets. There are masses of categorized mental illnesses that are documented in the enigmatic text known as the **DSM** (the Diagnostic Statistical Manual). The DSM is a manual that categorizes all the formulated mental illnesses. It has been routinely updated, recently arriving at its fifth edition, and it is a collaborative work of those in the field of psychiatry and psychology. The DSM categorizes what are believed to be all the existing mental illnesses and it lists the criteria that are to be met to assign a particular illness to a particular individual. The DSM is universally known in its field and it addresses all the formulated mental illnesses. It is a highly controversial manual and often is of great critical interest to practitioners. There are multitudes of criticisms of the DSM, and most rightly so. The diagnostic criteria of the DSM universally lack the gold standard of rigorous scientific validity and therefore diagnostics slip into clinical subjectivity. However, the DSM is currently the most pertinent text on the phenomena we call mental illness.

The criticisms of the DSM have been persistent over decades and will continue for as long as the DSM is the prominent and most influential text in the field. The issues with the DSM are complex and much has been written about its deficits and controversies. But at this point, I believe, the DSM-5 is the best we have in terms of the descriptors of mental illness. Interestingly, if one looks at the first DSM compared to the current edition, one will notice great variance. This is not overly surprising as over time subjective concepts can certainly be refined and reinterpreted. The DSM provides diagnostic codes to the formulated pathologies or mental illnesses. If you are curious of the diagnostic code for schizophrenia it is known as 295.90. Another most interesting nuance pertaining to the DSM is that a competent professional could likely provide a diagnosis of a mental illness to 100% of the of the population over the course of an individual's lifetime except for infants and toddlers. This is not to say that all mental illnesses are on par with one another. Certainly, some diagnostic phenomenon can be far more severe, debilitating, and intrusive compared to others. My intent is not to get into all the issues and controversies of the DSM as it is certainly a hornet's nest as all those in the field will attest. Nevertheless, the DSM does offer much needed information and can be highly pragmatic. But most assuredly it should be understood in its proper context.

The DSM is a lengthy volume refined over decades that is fastidiously dedicated to the categorization (kudos to Aristotle, the master of categorization) and descriptions of mental illness. And all the while, many a learned men and women still disagree as to the validity of mental illness as a truism let alone to the defined categories and descriptions to its associated phenomena. Some individuals disavow mental illness as factual. In support of this position, one may posit that rather than the given descriptor of mental illness the phenomena that presents in some individuals is just a different human experience from the norm. Rather than the attribution of the label termed as mental illness, such individual outlier presentations could otherwise be benignly described as uncustomary and with associated behaviors, thoughts, and moods outside of normative conceptions. Such a contrarian may posit alternative explanations exclusive to the term of mental illness including, for example, explanations based more on a spiritual context or perhaps a **quantum worldview**. The concept of mental illness is particularly provocative to varying viewpoints, including those that are quite divergent. But what else should one expect from such a complex concept? Some believe in the concept of mental illness and others do not. Nevertheless, we persist, my dear reader, still yet undeterred for reconciliation is but a matter of perspective.

I have been attributed the label of Schizophrenia, paranoid type. In general, as a diagnosis, it is considered a significant and debilitative disease indicative of a **thought disorder**. When one looks at the symptoms of schizophrenia as presented by the DSM, I have most readily experienced most if not all the symptoms. Currently, I am not going to look up the DSM and list the symptoms. I well know the referenced symptoms, but I eschew a verbatim dictate. Rather, I am going to write off-the-cuff about some of my experiences and how they are viewed as psychiatric symptoms. And please remember, I will be using established psychological terminology to express the symptoms. There is no need to patronize. Psychological verbiage has developed over the many centuries in description of certain human experiences and in description of certain human behaviors. I will use the appropriate terms as it is best to call that which is by its inherent name. The symptoms that I will be describing are symptoms that may be shared by other individuals with similar diagnostic criteria. Nevertheless, although there are commonalities as far as symptoms, I think it would be foolish to extrapolate that common symptoms equals identical experience. For it is my contention that my personal experience is uniquely mine although admittedly there may be some common themes to my experience that relate to the experiences of others.

8

Paranoid Schizophrenia

Firstly, a bit on what the diagnosis of Schizophrenia, paranoid type relates. Mental illness can be crudely divided, at least in part, by the concepts of mood versus thought. Disorders of mood are said to be "affective" disorders. Affective is a term indicating the concept of mood. Within the affective disorders, one will find such diagnostics as major depression, persistent depressive disorder, seasonal affective disorder, bipolar disorder, anxiety disorder, postpartum depression, and panic disorder amongst the many others. And by manner of brevity and as a matter of dalliance, I offer a quick tangent on the diagnostic of panic disorder. Panic disorder phenomenologically indicates repeated experiential states of panic. Typically, panic equates to an active fight-or-flight response inclusive to its correlates of fear, cortisol, and adrenaline. If you have ever seen an individual having a panic attack it can be a lurid observation. Having regular panic attacks is a certain life trial. But I now digress and return to diagnoses classified by mood (affective) versus diagnoses classified by disorders of thought. Thought disorders consist of diagnoses such as schizophrenia and psychotic disorders along with some overlap in certain **personality disorders**. The prefix "schizo" in Latin refers to "thought" and when one sees the prefix "schizo" it can be deduced to indicate issues with non-normative thought. The boundaries between thought disorders and mood disorders are not firm lines of exclusivity but rather are somewhat permeable and are, in a manner, coexistent on a complex spectrum, or at least in part. Nevertheless, the distinction between mood disorders and thought disorders is a valuable delineation in understanding many diagnostics, although admittedly, my offering is formulated in a most general and rudimentary manner.

Regarding the linguistic term "schizo" and how relates to the concept of mental illness, I offer a few pertinent items for consideration. As I previously wrote, many a learned men and women argue that mental illness as a concept is but a psychological misnomer. In this vein, consider for a moment the term schizo and the meaning behind the term. Again, "schizo" indicates a disorder of thought. For a moment, then, consider the expression "a disorder of thought" and then consider the argument that mental illness does not exist. How can an individual have a disorder of thought? Thoughts are thoughts and to judiciously delineate that some individuals have thoughts that are chronically pathological is an argument in favor of the premise of "proper thought" versus "improper thought." How can an arbitrary committee of professionals, including psychiatrists, psychologists, and social workers, lay claim to a delineation that some thoughts are pathological while others are not? This is a very slippery slope and when considered prima facie, it is absurd. Thoughts are simply thoughts and to label specified thoughts as disordered is indeed a murky enterprise. A rather plausible argument, don't you think? But my intent is not in pertinence of whether mental illness exists or it does not. Rather, my efforts are to deconstruct the term mental illness for the moment and give it some consideration. But for purposes of an astute clarity, my perspective and opinion rests firmly and securely of the assertion that mental illness does in fact exist by manner of specified types and by course of variable presentations. Mental illness is a complex concept and I find issues of mental illness to present on a broad spectrum with many variables to consider. When conceptualizing or diagnosing mental illness, it is best evaluated from a comprehensive gestalt or from a macro perspective rather than from a firmly differentiated typical yes/no binary derivative.

Returning to the symptoms of my diagnostic label of Schizophrenia, paranoid type, the following is a list, in part, of some of the symptoms I have experienced over time. Again, my intent is not to list the symptoms as strictly derivative from the DSM, but rather just an off-the-cuff summary based on recollections and not necessarily fully comprehensive or exhaustive. Remember, I am using the linguistic terms that have been established over time from the fields of psychiatry and psychology. To begin, some of the symptoms I have experienced include **auditory hallucinations**, feelings of paranoia, and **delusions**. The conglomerate of these symptoms is referred to as "psychosis." Psychosis is a term used to refer to the phenomenon of being detached from "reality." The term reality, as one may imagine, can quickly muddy the waters as far as what is in fact reality and what is in fact not reality. From the clinical viewpoint, explaining reality is best understood by an example. Consider the following. In our lives, we interact and share with one another in a mostly logical manner with a mostly linear progression that more or less makes sense to its participants. The characteristics of this shared reality are marked by traits of rationality including by form and content of conversation. Also, one can expect a fairly consistent range of human behavior in the context of the day. This shared reality between you and me, and of the larger group and population, is a "**socially constructed reality.**" Social construction procedurally evolves from our interactions with one another as predicated on "tacit agreement."

I earlier spoke of tacit agreement in furtherance of the following conceptualization. This next ideational item is an extremely important consideration when conceptualizing reality. The tacit agreement regarding our socially constructed expectations of one another largely creates our shared reality. It truly is amazing how much of our tacitly agreed upon, socially constructed reality is often taken for granted. When one walks out the front door of one's home, with that exit, many expectations are present in our psychology albeit mostly at a subconscious level. One quick example will illustrate the notion of a shared reality. Five individuals stand near a flagpole with the USA flag waving above. All five agree the flag is on the flagpole, as they so plainly observe. Five out of five agree, and therefore, a mutually shared, socially constructed, and tacitly agreed-upon reality will easily unfold for all its participants. All is well with the shared reality. Contrarily, however, in the same scenario, four out of the five of the individuals agree about the flag on the pole but the fifth disagrees with the four, and instead reports seeing a towel that is waving in the wind. So now what? What is the reality of the situation?

The difference of opinion of the sole individual has created some doubt as to the actual reality although the four that see the flag on the pole are quite confident about the content of their reality. After all, there is strength in numbers. In this scenario, the four agree on the flag as their shared reality and the single individual is left puzzled. This is not exactly a very important scenario, but I think it capably conveys the idea. Now even further into this scenario, consider the lone individual who saw the towel and not the flag. If this same individual continues to repeatedly and consistently contradict the tacitly agreed-upon socially constructed reality of others, over a course of time and in different social contexts, this individual may be viewed as having issues with reality. And further, depending on specified speech and behavior, such an individual may ultimately come to be viewed as medically psychotic. In a manner, this is a way to explain the term psychotic or psychosis- i.e., as a regular break or disconnection from so-called reality. I also want to add, that this example is very superficial and there are many other variables to consider when judging if someone is psychotic or experiencing psychosis. Generally speaking, however, there is a breakdown in the individual's conception of what is true and real as opposed to the more uniformed and agreed-upon reality of the masses.

Many phenomena other than psychosis can also be explained by a breakdown in the populous' shared reality. Oftentimes the breakdown occurs across cultures. The Nazis, for example, and I know this topic is highly and appropriately sensitive, communed in a collectively agreed-upon reality based on the ideology of **eugenics**. This collective Nazi psychology had momentum for a time but ultimately the reality shifted, and thankfully so, into a saner and more humane reality (but only after significant warfare). Another example to consider is that of suicide bombers. The actions of a suicide bomber are almost unfathomable to the masses and are not consistent with our larger collective reality. And lastly, consider the "lone wolf gunman" who opens fire at a school or mall (and all my sensitivities go out to such victims) and later is found to have a history of mental health issues including perhaps issues with psychosis. If closely examined, many phenomena can be explained by a breakdown in our fragile shared reality. Such occurrences happen daily (often in the news) and can be easily observed if given specified attention.

Psychosis is a medical term used to indicate a clinically significant incongruence between the afflicted individual's sense of reality versus that of the unafflicted collectivity. Upon observation, one will find that some human phenomena can be best explained by the fragile breakdown of the collective social fabric while alternatively other human phenomena can be best explained by the attribute of psychosis. Both possibilities reflect breakdowns in reality but with highly differentiated explanations. An individual with schizophrenia who is actively and intrusively symptomatic over time and in various social contexts, is an individual that could be labeled as medically "psychotic" and currently pathological. Symptoms such as auditory hallucinations, **mind-reading, ideas of reference, thought broadcasting**, delusions, and paranoia can together create an individual whom may be described as actively psychotic and therefore "not in touch with reality." It is paramount to understand that the experiences of the psychotic individual are certainly real to that individual, but in no manner are the experiences considered rational by others or as characteristic of the collective reality.

What is the experience of psychosis like, and specifically, what is it like in my personal experience? To answer this question adequately, I must first digress to some of my psychiatric history. My issues with psychosis over the last twenty plus years thankfully has been intermittent, or another words, my issues have come and gone and have proved not to be consistently persistent at all times and over time. In my experiences with psychosis, let me explain a few important details. Firstly, the initial episode of my psychosis, in my early twenties, was psychologically very disturbing, and additionally was tremendously disruptive to all aspects and realms of my life. Why was this so? Well, in a general sense, the **first onset of psychosis** in most individuals often is the most problematic. The primary issues with the first onset psychosis are two-fold. Firstly, when the first onset of psychosis occurs, the great majority of the time, the individual has no insight, understanding, or knowledge of the presentation of the illness and its symptoms. Ignorance, in this case, certainly proves not to be bliss! Returning to my personal case history, as a young man at twenty years old or thereabouts, I was considered sane, rational, and well in tune with the elements of shared reality. Now enter the variables of mental illness and psychosis. Most curiously, in the disorder of schizophrenia, the onset of the disorder usually occurs in the age range of approximately 18 to 24. This is when the illness's initial presentation often occurs. I find this trait of the illness unusual but such it is. So there I was, a recent university graduate, psychologically well, and actively pursuing career goals. I was living alone in an apartment and I was pursuing a career in broadcasting. I was also working part-time in a supermarket to help pay the rent. I was twenty-one. I was sane, rational, and without any psychological disturbances. Then, without warning and with no preparation, comes the initial onset of psychosis.

Firstly, let me explain a bit about the pertinent issue regarding what is clinically termed the "first onset of psychosis." The issue of the first onset of psychosis is a very important issue when understanding psychosis in its totality. In my instance, the first onset of psychosis was not an overnight phenomenon. It was not like I woke up one day and I was thoroughly psychotic. What did happen, rather, was more of the following. Over a period of about a year, various symptoms crept slowly into my psychology and intellect. The symptoms of paranoia, delusions, auditory hallucinations, mind-reading, ideas of reference, and thought broadcasting slowly and very subtly introduced themselves into an otherwise rational psychology. In pertinence of these symptoms, let me briefly explain the definitions along with some examples.

Paranoia is likely understood in a general sense by most. But in relation to schizophrenia, the experience is not merely a generic feeling. Clinical paranoia can be disabling and it is intrusively disturbing. I can describe the clinical paranoia experience by the following example, at least in part. Firstly, do you remember that feeling when riding a steep roller coaster and the coaster gains speed and hurriedly takes its downward dive? Do you know that feeling when your stomach seems to drop as the coaster speedily descends? When I experience paranoia, it usually begins with that feeling in my stomach, that immediate sinking feeling like when descending a coaster. Along with the feeling, the thoughts that follow usually are along the lines of "this is not good; this is very bad; this is trouble; I am in danger; this cannot be happening; what have I done to deserve this?" From this point, the paranoia along with its associated thoughts, seeps in my psychology to a visceral intensity and I succumb to a status cognitive agita. The feeling is not of being a little suspicious or a little ill at ease, rather, it is much more profound and encompassing. During paranoid episodes, the feeling is intensely troublesome and disturbing. In my experience, paranoia is a feeling that is dark and horrifying, and perhaps most importantly, a feeling marked by hopelessness. It is a feeling of pervasive doom, and even at times a feeling of being, as a matter of fact, eternally damned. I think the linguistic choice of "eternal damnation" may be the best descriptor to the experience. The feeling of paranoia, and I write this without hyperbole and to be understood both literally and figuratively, possesses the qualities assumptive to the state of "Hell" itself. When highly paranoid, I have asked myself on more than one occasion if I was indeed literally in "Hell." This is not fun stuff, for sure, but I think it appropriately conveys the feeling of clinical paranoia at its intensity and apex. It moves well beyond a passing suspiciousness. The feeling can persist over time for hours, days, and sometimes months. It is a state of mind conducive to suicidality. And although suicide has never been more than a contemplation on my part at the same time, I can certainly understand other individuals with similar problems considering, and ultimately acting on, the impulse to self-harm. In my specified instance, however, I find this of no recourse or prevailing option. In this capacity I prefer God's will to my own.

The next typical symptom of a personal frequency are termed as auditory hallucinations. Auditory hallucinations, clinically abbreviated as AH, are the hearing of voices that are not heard, or that are not "auditory," to others also present in the same environment. A key aspect to understanding auditory hallucinations is the one experiencing the symptom definitively hears voices but others in the same environment hear nothing of the like. Usually, the voices

I hear sound as coming from the external environment rather than internally from my own mind. The voices are mostly horrifying and disturbing and are persistently derogatory and often penetrate my vulnerabilities. The voices contribute immensely to my feelings of paranoia. The voices trigger fight or flight and anxiolytic feelings. The voices can be frequent, intermittent, and/or occasional. In my experience, the content of the hallucinations oftentimes presents as the worst possible thing to be heard for that particular moment and for that particular situation. Once the auditory hallucinations begin to kick in and then persist over a period, they present with some range as far as their content and in ability to further provoke my disturbed mind. An interesting aspect to my auditory hallucinations is that after hearing the voices for a period they begin to integrate into my mind as parcel to my own cognitive functioning. In other words, they sort of become like my own thoughts after a while. After consistently hearing voices over time, they integrate, not wholly but certainly in part, into my own psychology. This is the tricky part for me. It becomes quite the task of insight to differentiate my own thoughts from auditory hallucinations. The whole process becomes arduous. I will speak more on auditory hallucinations later but for now I will move onto the symptom of "delusions."

The clinical definition of a delusion is that of an acquired "false belief." This definition sounds innocent and benign enough but delusions can be ravenous. My personal delusions, of which I have had multitudes too high to enumerate, generally revolve around core central themes. Those of whom share this psychotic symptom will likely experience delusions with similar overarching themes but at the same time delusions can be intensely personalized and individually specified. In the DSM, delusions are categorized into various subtypes based on typical themes. Some of the delusional subtypes include the grandiose, persecutory, somatic, and erotomanic. When I am under the influence or persuasion of a delusion, clinically speaking, I am experiencing and projecting a current belief about the specific situation, myself, or others that is in stark contrast to the larger tacitly agreed upon mutually socially constructed reality of the masses. When experiencing a delusion, the perception is real to me but in no way is part of the larger consensus reality. And thus, it becomes highly paradoxical. And mastering this paradox is the key to conquering schizophrenia. But more on this crucial item of paradox later.

All clinically differentiated delusional subtypes come with a generalized associated theme but at the same time any such delusional content can also be novel and unique from each to each. In pertinence of the various typified delusions that are categorized according to theme and trait, I offer the following personal exemplars for reasons of clarity and deeper understanding. My first personal example involves the grandiose. A specific grandiose delusion I once experienced was that I was in a friendship with the then President of the United States. This delusion was recurrent over time and was intermittent over a period of many years. The delusion was a product, in part, of hearing voices that I believed were that of the President of the United States. As far as experiencing grandiose delusions, over the many years of my illness, such delusions have been far more infrequent compared to other types of delusions, especially the type known as persecutory delusions. And as a sidebar, the grandiose delusion of being in a friendship with the President of the United States, after a brief period of time, ultimately turned persecutory in nature. So then, what are persecutory delusions and how do they fit in the totality of my personal experience?

Persecutory delusions are fallacious beliefs that are characteristically detrimental, adverse, and dystonic to the perceiving self. Over the course of my illness, I have been inundated with this symptom. I have had thousands of persecutory delusions. I have had more persecutory delusions than days in number. These types of delusions can be brief in time, can last minutes to hours, or can be more perseverative spanning days, weeks, months, or even years. As a clinical typified subtype, persecutory delusions involve the theme of perceptions of a personal persecution. In my case they arrive and persist accompanied by feelings of paranoia.

To explain how a persecutory delusion feels, I offer the analogy of the final days of Jesus Christ as an example. According to the Catholic Bible, Christ was physically nailed to a cross and left to perish as the culmination to his brutal persecution. Persecutory delusions are the mental equivalent of being physically nailed to the cross. I certainly do not wish to exploit the persecution of Christ in my explanation, but it does provide a descriptive analogy, and admittedly my example is hyperbolic as I certainly do not want to compare myself to the sufferings of Christ on the cross. Nevertheless, persecutory delusions are wrought with mental anguish. Persecutory delusions are marked by beliefs that others are deliberately trying to cause pain, suffering, humiliation, fear, and harm to me. The delusions feel as though others are trying to persecute me by their words and actions. When these delusions are present, I feel like I am often in a double-bind situation. In other words, I feel like there is no escape from the perceived dark and evil context of the situation. In terms of linguistics, I do not haphazardly choose the words "dark and evil." Oftentimes, in my experience, the delusions are perceptions of a pure form of evil intent. When experiencing such delusions, I often find asking myself "what have I ever done to deserve this?" The felt experience of being the target of deliberate executions of evil by others is no pedestrian perception. The delusions oftentimes feel as though they will persist over time, and even more disturbingly, they often feel as if I am situated in a perseverative, constant, and fixed reality that I will have to bear without relent. Persecutory delusions often feel hellish, intense, and indiscriminately punitive without capacity for solution and are experienced to be absent of any potential abatement. Persecutory delusions are perhaps the most difficult part of my illness. They are terribly disturbing and are facilitative to unimagined increments of mental anguish. Simply put, I hate and detest persecutory delusions. They are so very difficult.

I have had too many persecutory delusions to count and so many in number that recalling each and every experience, in all their nuances, is an impossibility for me. I do remember most of my psychotic experiences, both generally and at times specifically, but they are similar to all memories in that they can fade away in part over time. And truthfully, for my own sanity, they are better left forgotten. These experiences are often traumatic experiences and persecutory delusions often play a significant role in the horror. To provide an idea of the specific content of some of my persecutory delusions, I offer the following as some examples for consideration. It is best to remember that these examples were actual experiences. They are not passing thoughts. They are premises to experiences that persist over time. It is important to understand that they are felt experiences, believed to be true at the time, and as existing over time in varying durations. Each offering is largely a separate and unique delusion unto itself, although I am sure there are likely some overlaps in content. In my own terminology, I refer to each separate experienced delusion as an "episodic" experience. Such exemplary persecutory delusions include being used by the federal government in a manipulative ploy, having a microchip implanted in my brain when sleeping in order to control me, being lobotomized while asleep, being abducted by aliens and physically transplanted onto a different planet, being rejected by all other people including family as well as being rejected by God, believing others know all of my thoughts (more on this later), contemplations of actually being present in "Hell," the belief of being captured on live video for the rest of humanity to observe, and the belief that I am under remote control by others. These are but a few of the many. Such beliefs will emerge and recede, and will shuffle and shift, over an impetuous chronology and they will similarly share the common theme of perceptions of persecution. All these delusions are very difficult to experience. Some are more difficult than others. They all can be frightening.

Early in my illness, these types of delusions triggered me to behave in a highly erratic and irrational manners, and triggered intense feelings of utter hopelessness. Over the course of my illness, although still very arduous and challenging, managing such delusions is a bit less difficult due to their increasing familiarity and my increasing insight. Twenty some odd years into my illness the delusion of the microchip, for example, does not bother me as much as it once did. When I experience the recurrent microchip delusion, I now say to myself, for example and in part, that the microchip is a "possibility." And because of its recurrence and its now modest familiarity, I retort to myself that even if it is true, "I really do not care anymore." It's almost like it is analogous to a joke to me now. In other words, yes, it is possible but who cares? My ability to shrug off such a dire possibility for some reason amuses me much akin to a bad joke. Delusions certainly are not funny per se, as in an enjoyable manner of speaking, but I guess I have adopted a sense of humor as a means to coping. I have repeatedly found myself in such utter dire situations that living an existence on the brink of hopelessness has become familiar. And familiarity has become protective. From its characteristic repetition, I have effectively learned to mitigate the psychotic bite. And by and by, I have concluded by manner of score and vagabond that de facto all the psychotic chaos will eventually be personally relegated to the status of a mere cognitive chew. As such, from the darkened chaos emerges a lighted and ever-evolving insight. And with insight, all life items remain capably viable and psychosis returns to its inherent clandestine nature.

I think the most difficult persecutory delusional content I have endured is the recurrent episode of being rejected by all of humanity along with being rejected by God, as well. For where else is one to turn? All has been negated, and nothing is seemingly left as refuge. This delusion is frightening to experience, wrought with hopelessness, intense in presentation, and is the epitome of a sickening evil. Delusions are both cognitive and experiential. They are difficult to discard as simply extraneous or impertinent. These are intense experiences, but with familiarity and refined insight, being able to shrug off such dark experiences has become a well-earned cognitive ability. I used to ruminate, now I try to quickly discard. I say to myself, I may be in a form of hell, but I can still watch the Red Sox, take to the basketball court, and enjoy a short stack of blueberry pancakes. In other words, I continue to live my life with these certain pleasantries while simultaneously living in a world of perceived rejection. I don't know if it's just me and my sense of humor, but this dichotomized juxtaposition presents as amusing to my mind, at least in part, and so I shrug off the delusion and attempt to forget about it, at least for the moment. The familiarity of such repetitious dire situations has proven to be an apparent vulnerability of the illness and in furtherance of my ability to cope. In a sense, with familiarity comes some comfort. But in all honesty, until my dying day (more on death later), I do not think I will know with any absolute clarity whether such possibilities are in fact the "truth." The promising aspect for me, however, is that I am now able to persist in my life and its activities even given such dire backdrops. But in all candor, what alternative do I have? We all must play the hand we are dealt.

Now, more briefly, I'd like to just finish in describing some of the other types of categorized delusions, those being, somatic delusions and **erotomanic delusions**. Somatic delusions are false beliefs concerning one's body. An example of a somatic delusion could be an individual of the belief that he had no stomach, when in fact he had no medical issues concerning his stomach. Or perhaps, the erroneous belief that one had a disease, say cancer, that was medically disproven as fact. Nevertheless, individuals could persist in their delusions and believe they were living with cancer when in fact there would be no medical evidence. Erotomanic delusions consist of beliefs of romantic involvements and/or relationships with others that are in fact nonexistent and unconstituted. Such delusions are usually centered on someone famous and prominent. For example, and erotomanic delusion may consist of individuals believing that they are romantically involved with a celebrity. These people sometimes make the entertainment news as "stalkers" of the celebrity. At times, they may indeed be stalkers, but at other times, the behavior may be better explained and understood as derivative of delusional thinking. I have had a few erotomanic type delusions, and, just for fun, I will mention the belief I briefly held of being in a relationship with the pop star Madonna (lol). In my experience, my erotomanic delusions have been very brief in time and very minimal in number. My erotomanic delusions also have not been causal to significant suffering or distress, and in fact, were briefly enjoyable. But, like all other delusions, they too have come to pass. In summary, the prominent type of delusions I have experienced are those of the persecutory type. I have also experienced grandiose, somatic, and erotomanic delusions but those have been far fewer in number and far more transient in time. There are other clinical categorical types of delusions as well, but such delusions have not played much of a role in the experience of my illness. So at this point, further elucidation on typified delusions is not overly pertinent. Perhaps another time. But if you are truly curious, just look them up in the DSM (or perhaps on this thing we call the internet! lol!).

Before returning to specific experienced symptoms, some salience is required pertaining to my "schizo" disorder. In general, when these symptoms first presented, during the time frame of the first onset of psychosis and shortly thereafter, they were intensely disturbing and powerfully debilitating to my ability to function. Over the many years of the illness, however, and the longer I live with the disorder, the more I can thoughtfully process the symptoms and understand my experiences as secondary to the causal effects of pathological phenomena, and in doing so, I have been able to mediate their debilitating effects, at least to some degree. Over the many years of this illness, the repetitive commonness of the symptoms over long periods of time has led me to improved personal insight. I have learned, even while highly symptomatic, to keep my behavior under tight control. Early in in the illness, the symptoms triggered me to engage in tremendously erratic, irrational, and bizarre behavior. Such behavior, along with my illogical and irrational use of language, caused repeated psychiatric hospitalizations. My behavior and speech were significantly out of concert with the consensus reality. Returning to the present, now when I experience various symptoms, I have familiarity with the generalized persecutory content and of the types of experiences that can be triggered by such symptoms. The symptoms are thematically familiar to me, at least in part and in the simplest of terms, rather than presenting to me as eerily novel and completely disarming as they once were during the initial onset time frame. At this point in my illness, even when highly symptomatic, including having symptoms of auditory hallucinations, paranoia, delusions, and various other symptoms, I have learned to monitor my behavior, language, and conversations and I make damn well sure that I am remaining as rational as is humanly possible given the presence of multiple symptoms. Many years ago and during the first couple years of the illness, multiple symptoms triggered highly irrational, erratic, and inappropriate behavior and speech including behaving and speaking dramatically out of proper social context. Twenty plus years into the illness, now while I'm experiencing multiple symptoms, I have a definite strategy. I now closely monitor, observe, and regulate my behavior and my conversations, and I make sure that I am acting as rationally, routine, and of the mindset of "minding my own business" while doing my best to engage in "everyday" behaviors, including engaging in benign and superficial conversations. I monitor my behavior, actions, and words for reasons of personal sustenance. Doing this allows me to continue to function as an ordinary citizen. It allows me to work, drive, do my errands, socialize, and in general participate in the consensus reality of society. During the early years of the illness, multiple symptoms created devastating life consequences, including hospitalizations, poor social functioning, confusion, and emotional distress including feelings of hopelessness and terror. Now the symptoms, although still disturbing, unwanted, and adversely powerful are at least common enough to my experience that I can continue to function. I am acting the part and I am faking it until I make it. This is the only way to manage the illness. I cannot make the pathological symptoms cease altogether, but I can control my behaviors and conversations. As such, the symptoms are not quite as debilitating as they once were. All the psychological chaos has become a known quantity and I have acclimated. In other words, I am kind of used to it all at this point.

I have concluded that my personal experiences are grounded in reality, but just not wholly inclusive to consensus reality. This purview assists because it legitimizes my personal experiences but also places them appropriately in the context of the greater consensus reality. Additionally and importantly, although certain adverse realities present as true to my mind at a specific time, the particular experience inevitably recedes into the past tense and ultimately evaporates into an otherwise inert delusional wasteland along with the vast others. In other words, the old adage of "this too shall pass" is indeed the coping means I use regardless of the dark, disturbing, debilitating, persecutory, and evil experiences I endure. They all do come to pass. Sometimes the dark experiences will last hours, days, weeks, and even months at times without relent. But thus far, they all have thankfully relinquished given enough time and given enough personal faith that it is only a terrible dream that will eventually pass and go away. I must have conviction that I will endure, and I must use my insight into the madness to allow me to continue to function. If the symptoms did not relent over time and remained constant, I do not think I could manage in any kind of effective utilitarian manner. If the symptoms did not relent, I think I would have to take a permanent vacation from society and perhaps go live on a farm and commune with the animals and perhaps have an occasional come to pass with a neighbor! Seriously, though, if the symptoms did not eventually come to pass, my behavior would once again be subject to questioning by consensus society. On the other hand, I have played a hand when my chips are down before so perhaps I would survive and find sustenance by method of some novel manneristic Tao. I have had evil experiences that have persisted for months and during these times I feel like I am holding on by a thread. Sometimes I feel like I can barely breathe, or take another step, and I feel like there is no possible way to engage with others in any type of normalized fashion. I feel out of control and my experiences are consistently and persistently persecutory. The best descriptor of these experiences for me is evil. I feel exhausted, and I feel like there's no possible way to endure during these times. My existence feels blocked in all directions, paths, and manners. I have no perceived path of effective functioning or of ultimate escape. My experiences present as evil, pure evil. But I also conjure, is not the experience of evil possible? Indeed, it may be so. But what I know with certainty, however, is that the aforementioned thread I often find myself hanging onto has thus far has been sufficient...and I wonder if a thread is all that is required after all.

I will now return to the description of my symptoms and how they relate to my felt experiences. There are two prominent symptoms I would like to discuss. The first being "thought broadcasting" and the second being "mind-reading." This is the clinical verbiage pertaining to these symptoms. Thought broadcasting and mind-reading are quite similar in their presentation. Both are arduous and exhausting and make experiences very difficult to manage. These symptoms very effectively create a perceived psychological vulnerability in my relation to others. Both symptoms can trigger and sustain multitudes of different delusions by manner of inherent characteristic. Thought broadcasting is a term used to describe the phenomenon of thinking that others in the environment, all others in the environment, can literally hear my thoughts verbatim. It is the belief that the thoughts I am having are being "broadcasted" to all others in earshot. Thusly, the experience of thought broadcasting is believing that all those around me are privileged to the exact content of my thoughts. Therefore, whatever I am thinking is known, in exactitude and verbatim, to those with whom I am present. Therefore, any thought that I would prefer to be private has no such privacy. As one may imagine, this experience could be very disconcerting, including experiencing feelings of vulnerability and powerlessness. Most importantly, in regard to this symptom, the experience is not mutual. In other words, I do not have any experience of hearing the thoughts of others. It is a one-way pattern. If it were reciprocal, perhaps it would be more manageable and a more level playing field, but it is not so. The term broadcasting is a useful term as a descriptor in relaying the general idea of the concept and symptom. In further differentiation, the symptom is not of the like of a loud bullhorn announcements projected into the environment. Rather, it is more like a telepathic-like conduit to others. Along with the obvious vulnerability created by such a perceived situation, I also experience a self-loathing, for I come to perceive my own mind as defective and incapable of its own self-control. With this symptom I perceive my thoughts as entirely public and I have no sense of cognitive privacy. My thoughts become consumptive by all and intense feelings of persecution ensue. My perceptions indicate that others are much obliged to simply relax, hear my thoughts, and to be ever so grateful that they are not the doomed soul in my situation. On the other hand, however, enters the characteristic schizophrenic paradox for my cumulative insight indicates that others in fact cannot hear my thoughts. This I am sure because the symptom is transient over time. However, when I experience the symptom, the perception is real and the experience is real. Without personal privacy in your thoughts, vulnerability certainly will emerge. And with those vulnerabilities comes feelings of paranoia and persecution. Certainly, a most uncomfortable symptom.

The clinical term "mind-reading" is yet another personally prominent experiential symptom. It has some similarities to thought broadcasting in its presentation. When I experience the symptom of mind-reading the phenomenon is a bit more of a two-way process rather than the one-way flow of thought broadcasting. The symptom of mind-reading is the experience of conversations between my mind and the minds of others without the necessary use of overt or spoken language. It is communication between my mind and the mind of others with whom I am present. Usually, after a temporally brief experience in the two-way nature of mind-reading, the symptom often morphs into thought broadcasting and as such the directional flow of communication characteristically resorts to the unilateral pattern or modality. Initially upon its arrival, I will view mind-reading proper as an absurd impossibility and as an inert passing intellectual novelty. But once the symptom persists for hours, days, or weeks its experiential provocations become increasingly familiar. With its temporal persistence, my intellect eventually succumbs to its perceived veracity and consequently mind to mind communication emerges as a legitimate manner for valid discourse. Once believed, the singular symptom mutates by manner into the greater delusional form and my reality is yet again recreated. When in retrospect and cognitively panning for valuable nuggets of golden insight, I always marvel at how an isolated symptom can transform to delusional status given its recurrence over time mixed with an ample voracity. I suppose for these are but the ingredients to the delusional countenance.

When trying to cope with the symptom of mind-reading, I will often self-talk "Robert, you cannot communicate mind to mind; stop this nonsense!" But nevertheless, the experience will persist. Then, adding to my commentary, I will say to myself, "well, Robert, it is possible. After all, you are experiencing it." I frequently use the framing of "possibilities" when attempting to banish irksome symptoms. Therefore, by manner of proper logic, when I view mind-reading as a legitimate possibility of consensus reality the symptom then at the same time must also be subject to "not possibility." If it is possible and not possible at the same time, then logically I can cognitively stash it for the time being as a "not possibility." In this manner, I am coping in accordance to a Zen perspective. And I reiterate when conquering schizophrenia, it is paramount to always remember it is primarily a metaphysical and paradoxical disease. Therefore, when I cognitively process the symptom and psychologically reframe it as both possible and not possible, it seems to lessen the intensity and it seems to mediate the detrimental effects. And gratefully thus far, and like the rest of my symptoms, this symptom too has come to pass. Once my symptoms abate, a sense of normalcy returns accompanied by a most welcoming **tabula rasa** and I begin anew as again unfettered. That is, at least for the time being!

There are a few more symptoms inclusive to the "schizo" disorders I would like address. It is not my intent to describe all the symptoms in full detail as I think that would eventually prove boring and overly mechanical. And in pertinence to the topical of mechanical writing, and in lieu of creativity over predictable textual enumeration, I offer a brief pivot from the heavy to lighted and in regards to the procedural elements of a routinized writing style. The inherent nature to writing involves a logical progression and as such writing customarily contains an intrinsic flaw. Writing can become overly mechanical. In other words, in fulfillment of the idea one may be writing about, the text becomes predictable in its linear progression. For example, someone might be writing on the topic of "The Civil War." Now, there are many ways to present the idea of the Civil War but methodologically what usually happens is something approximate to the following exemplary linear progression: Chapter 1 – The Years Before the Civil War; Chapter 2- Disagreements Between the North and South; Chapter 3- The Early Battles; Chapter 4-The Middle Battles; Chapter 5- The Turning Point, and linearly so on and so forth. See the mechanical nature of the book? And although I love books, this has always been an aspect that disinterests me. I can pick up a book, read its title, look at the table of contents, and definitively know the flow of the text from page one to the last. I will know exactly where the text was headed, and quite frankly, after reading the foreword (and by the way, always read the foreword as it will be crucial to the text) and chapter 1, my patience for the body of the text greatly wanes and I find myself reading just to get to the end of the already intuited linear progression. To me, interesting ideas are not simply linear. I find most nonfiction books tersely linear. An otherwise lively psychedelic idea becomes manipulated, chopped, and segmented by form linear and process mechanical. Once the idea becomes sequentially churned and detailed, a zippy conclusion is offered and the text is complete. The text can then be jacketed and the idea henceforth takes the tangible book form markedly and characteristically as a linear work subject to the traditional conception of the book ideal. I have a displeasure for this type of progression. In my mind, ideas are much too beautiful to bludgeoned in total into a comprehensively linear and mechanical form. Ideas by their very nature are nonlinear, non-chronological, and more of a conglomeration of thoughts united by common themes. Ideas connect a number of thoughts that superficially may have no connection. I view ideas similarly to Plato's conception of the "**forms**." I see ideas as ideals. So, I thank you for allowing this nonlinear insertion into my otherwise linear and logical writing. I felt this nonlinear insertion compulsory. We can now return to regular programming, that currently being, my thoughts on mental illness and its symptoms. And with a contented satiety, my dear reader, thus ends my dalliance and diversion.

In concluding my discussion regarding the symptomatology I have experienced, I will finish by detailing some "negative" generalized symptoms and then lastly, the specific symptom of "**thought blocking**." The terms "**negative symptoms**" and "thought blocking" are the utilized clinical verbiage. Negative symptoms present in a more passive manner than the previously described positive symptoms and as secondary and resultant of the experience of the positive symptoms. Negative symptoms in "schizo" type disorders include issues with affect (emotional climate) and **amotivation**. Affect is a descriptor indicating the generalized status of one's presenting emotional loci. Understood more vernacularly, affect is one's emotional "climate," while mood, on the other hand, is more like the current and acute "weather." Affect is more of a generalized sentiment. In "schizo" disorders, there are two primary types of issues with affect, those being in clinical verbiage "incongruent affect" and "**flat affect**." **Incongruent affect** is a descriptor used to indicate a mismatch between what is being spoken and the corresponding underlying mood that comes with the spoken content. The presentation of these two aspects can be incongruent, or other words they do not logically match one another. An example will clarify. An individual with an incongruent affect may say something of the like, "I'm sorry for your loss," as if at a wake or a funeral, but all the while the individual may be smiling or grinning with the statement. The content and the affect are incongruent. They do not logically match. As another example, consider an individual whom may be speaking to his therapist and reports, "I've never been happier," but all the while when speaking the individual is frowning and presents as emotionally sullen and sad. It is an incongruence of the spoken content and its underlying affect. The great comedian Steven **Wright** is a perfect example of someone with an incongruence between mood and spoken content (if you don't know Steven Wright and are looking for an example of incongruent affect, just YouTube him, and his schtick is a perfect example). Steven Wright's stand-up routine is predicated on the incongruence of his words and his affect. The clinical verbiage of incongruent affect, therefore, has explanatory utility in describing a disconnect between one's language and one's emotional climate. From such a presentation, it can be clinically inferred that one's thoughts are out of context with one's feelings and that one's thoughts are likely out of context with the general decorum and proceedings of the presenting social environment. Over the course of my illness, I have had my issues with incongruent affect. The most important aspect about incongruent affect in my experience is that it is not a symptom, in and of itself, that is particularly distressing much like the others. An incongruent affect is more of a clinical indicator of an existing thought disorder rather than an experientially distressing specified symptom. The presence of an incongruence results from the underlying pathological thinking along with an illogical emotional corollary. Trained mental health professionals can readily observe an incongruent affect and it is a good indicator to them of a possible thought disorder. Therefore, the symptom is not particularly distressing, but rather is a good clinical indicator. Once it is seen and observed it is more easily understood.

I will now move on to the negative symptom clinically termed as "flat affect." As a reminder, anytime the word affect is used in psychology, it is in reference to issues of one's broad emotional climate. Flat affect, therefore, is somewhat self-explanatory in that one's affect presents as both literally and figuratively "flat." Using the term flat is meant to convey a specific emotional presentation often present in "schizo" disorders. Flat affect is characterized by a statically expressionless drawn and sullen face. Although all people at times have expressionless faces, when one observes a flat affect it is a differentiated presentation compared to a more neutral mood or a more resting expressionless face. When one directly observes a flat affect, it is more readily understood. It is the expression of expressionless. A flat affect is also a good indicator of the lack of, or poverty of, thought activity. A flat affect correlates very well with the clinical term and symptom of a "**poverty of thought.**" Poverty of thought is a clinical term used to describe the lack of thoughts over time. Poverty of thought oftentimes presents simultaneously with another symptom termed "**poverty of speech.**" Poverty of speech is the clinical term used to describe a hyperbolic lack of spoken communication. The combination of poverty of thought and poverty of speech often present as part of the negative symptomatology of "schizo" disorders. The presence of these two symptoms, along with a flat affect, may present in an individual in the behavioral form of one sitting for hours, expressionless, and without use of spoken language. By manner, it can be a prelude to **catatonic behavior,** at least in part. In the experience of my "schizo" illness, all three of these symptoms have at one time or another been active. To this day, I cannot elude an affective flatness. I behaviorally compensate when in a social context but when alone there is no escape. Flatness has an unmistaken gravitational feel producing a drawn facial expression accompanied by feelings of a persistent sullenness. I also experience issues with poverty of thought and poverty speech, and when these two symptoms accompany a flat affect, I feel substantially "zoned out," mildly depressed, and it causes me to want to isolate and not be around others. Emotional flattening feels like a mild depression. The negative symptoms of flat affect, poverty of thought, and a poverty of speech are not as debilitating or disturbing compared to the positive symptoms. The negative symptoms are more secondary to the causal power of the positive symptoms. My experience of the negative symptoms mostly feels like a statically low mood that feels resistant to change, along with pervasive and lasting feelings of a psychic nothingness. The felt experience of the negative symptoms seems to mostly occur when the positive symptoms abate for the time being. During these time periods, my thought content seems to drain and empty of the frenetic and energetic pathological positive symptoms as I transition into the dulling abyss of the negative symptoms. And with the negative symptoms comes a thick sullenness accompanied by austere feelings of nothing but nothingness.

Emotional flattening, in my experience, also often coincides with the symptom clinically termed as "thought blocking." Thought blocking as a symptom often coincides with the symptoms of a poverty of thought and a poverty of speech. Thought blocking is an extremely frustrating symptom that affects my ability to think clearly and to speak clearly. It is the state of having no flow or succession to one's thoughts. In my experience, there is a pervasive feel of a cognitive nothingness. My thoughts are efficiently blocked and absent. It is an existence over time with very little cognitive fodder. It is a state of diminished psychological activity without adequate reprise. Its primary effect is that it inhibits my communication abilities. It also becomes difficult altogether to get a natural flow of thoughts moving once again. It is the analogous equivalent of your brain being stuck in concrete. I experience this symptom often and with it simple conversations become burdensome and an ensuing frustration capably percolates. This symptom is a nuisance.

The last negative symptom I will describe is "amotivation." Thought disorders can often lead to a generalized lack of gainful activity for the afflicted individual. Those with thought disorders often do not consistently persevere in regular work and social activity. Thought disorders often lead to quite sedentary lives. Individuals often can lose motivation in their activities of daily living, including at times, even hygienic issues. For me, regular physical and cognitive activity are part of my coping strategy. I often have to will myself to engage in activity, but once engaged in my habitual activities, amotivation as a symptom generally loses its causal efficacy. In my experience, amotivation was more of a presence at the initial onset of the illness. At this point, amotivation is low on my list of problem symptoms due in part to my primary strategy to always stay involved, active, and "in the game" as best I can regardless of current symptoms.

In summary, I have provided an overview of some of the negative symptoms of thought disorders that I personally experience. Prior to my description of the negative symptoms, I described the positive symptoms that occur in my mental illness, i.e., auditory hallucinations, paranoia, delusions, thought broadcasting and mind-reading. The combination of both the positive and negative symptoms contribute to the sum of the illness. The illness is characterized by multiple symptoms that persist over time and vary over time in cacophonic combinations. The felt experience of these schizo symptoms tangibly affects my life in all its inherent realms.

So, it is such, I must persist given multiple typical symptoms with permeable and cumulative life effects. But here I do not heed for this is no safe Eden for a psychological resting. Therefore, in consideration of my next chess move, I dutifully return to proper questions while seeking my refuge. My leading question emanates from the philosophical. Given said symptoms, therefore, how may I use these cognitive items while formulating an agreeable and preservative existential perspective? Upon this consideration, I offer that in the experience of my illness the totality vastly outweighs the sum of its parts. I emphasize that schizophrenia is extremely existential by its inherent nature. Its presence in my life has had overarching and fervent personal ramifications including shaping my conceptions about so-called reality. Schizophrenia has produced items of thought that otherwise would not have infiltrated my mind and psychology. This madness has had existential ramifications, at least as far as far as my personal experience is concerned. In a sense, schizophrenia has bruised my faculty of perception. Simply stated, I can no longer trust my perceptions. Schizophrenia is proof that perception does not always equate to reality. This being the case, I have learned to deny credence based in perception and I function by using other cognitive resources. I necessarily compensate so I may gainfully persist. I also find it helpful to every so often proclaim and attest, schizophrenia be damned!

9

Is a Madman a Safe Man?

In pertinence of prognostics and life outcomes, I want to detail a few most salient points. Firstly, if I did not have ample familial support it is entirely likely I would never have voluntarily became involved in mental health treatment inclusive of the use of prescription medication. I think it is very likely I could have slid into my personal madness and I would have persisted in such a mad state without any treatment or intervention. It is important to understand, and I believe this is a really important point, that when one is incrementally and very subtlety going mad, individuals on that descent, generally speaking, do not comprehend their own psychosis or their own emerging psychological pathology. Sometimes insight is altogether absent, and this is most especially true during the time of the first onset of psychosis and when there is a lack of caring social supports to provide the necessary feedback. The descent into madness is often subtlety incremental over time and in its subtlety the personal experience of the symptoms becomes obscured. In my experience, the gradual descent into a pervasive madness came with no personal inkling that perhaps this was all a result of a mental illness, or in the more vernacular, of just plain going "crazy." (I have no issue at all in using slang or vernacular terms in the description of my mental illness. I am not personally overly sensitive in this regard. The terms madness, mental illness, crazy, psychotic, nuts and insane all work for me.) When becoming mad in my early twenties, if I were on my own without any family or social supports, I believe my madness would have progressively and substantially worsened and in a most intense and intrusive manner. My functioning would have been pervasively debilitated, highly erratic, and significantly irrational, including regular behavior outside of social norms. And most importantly, I would have lacked any personal insight that I was in fact psychotic. Knowing you are in fact psychotic goes a long way in the recovery process. The ignorance and lack of awareness that one has progressed into a madness can unfortunately and commonly be catastrophic. In the experience of my illness, when it was first onset, I had an idea that my experience seemed to be changing from what I was accustomed. My experiences seemed to be off from my norm, but I rationalized that I was just experiencing life in its developmental progression. I was of the belief that I was experiencing the transition out of college and into the "real world." Never would I have made the self-assessment that I was in fact psychotic in the form of a schizo thought disorder. I just thought things were changing. I had not even the slightest of awareness that perhaps I was psychotic. The possibility never crossed my mind. I eventually learned, however, that mental illness is indiscriminate. Therefore, without family support and the necessary feedback regarding my behavior, I would have steadily descended into a deepening psychotic psychology. The outcome of this unchecked and rampant psychosis could have been permanently life-altering. In addition to potential legal issues, due to erratic public behavior, other probable possibilities may have included such outcomes as homelessness, the abject inability to work, potential safety issues both as a perpetrator or victim, incarceration, social isolation, poverty, poor diet and nutrition, issues of suicidality, and possible repeated long-term mandated psychiatric hospitalizations. Any combination of these outcomes is entirely plausible if not for having people around me that supported and helped me.

Around the time of the first onset of my illness, my family supports were confused about what was going on with me. Upon its initial occurrence, the family did not definitively proclaim "mental illness" with any sort of conviction. Mental illness was not something that was known to run in the family lineage and there was little family awareness of mental illness in general, including its permeable presentations. But my family supports did know that something just was not right with me. They knew I was off my norm and that my personality was altered. Thus began the learning curve for the family. It took about six months of my psychotic behavior, in total, before the family communed (without my knowledge), picked me up from my apartment, and took me to the hospital for an evaluation. I only agreed to go because I trusted my family (just a bit more than my own paranoia) and knew they had my best interest at heart even more so than my own skepticism of some type of pathology. I decided to go. I so clearly remember this day and having psychotic ideations in the car ride to the hospital. This family intervention, therefore, was my introduction to the mental health system and its treatment. Admittedly, however, this was not the beginning of a smooth and seamless transition into consistent and effective psychiatric treatment, but it was an initial introduction. It is not uncharacteristic for it to take multiple encounters with mental health services before a consistent adherence to treatment protocols is adopted and practiced by the afflicted individual. Additionally, for many others, regular engagement and adherence may be altogether avoided, or perhaps only practiced in part.

When one becomes psychotic and has little to no social support that can provide valuable feedback, oftentimes lives can be tragically affected. When I see the homeless person in ten layers of ragged clothing, unkempt, perhaps panhandling for money, and talking and mumbling to themselves, I often think of the quote, "There, but for the grace of God go I." Remember, when you see an impoverished or homeless individual on the streets talking, mumbling, and engaged in audible self-talk, this is a significant marker for the presence of a thought disorder. The clinical term for this linguistic behavior is "**self-dialoguing**," and it is often an indicator of mental illness. When I see the homeless phenomenon, I immediately think to myself it is very likely a product of an untreated thought disorder. Then immediately thereafter, I also think this could just as easily be me if not for my good fortune of reliable familial support. I consider myself to have no superior abilities only perhaps better luck. Unfortunately, untreated mental illness and deficient social support often correlates to poor life outcomes. This too lends explanation to the skewed ratio of homeless and incarcerated individuals with mental illness. These are the frequent adverse outcomes when social support is lacking.

Violence, including both harm-to-self and harm-to-others, is another potential adverse outcome of schizophrenia. Suicides, assaults, murders, and even killing sprees sadly can result from issues with mental illness especially when undiagnosed and untreated. These types of outcomes alter lives and in dramatic manners. It is important to understand, however, that those with severe mental illness who have been diagnosed and consistently engage in treatment protocols have no greater likelihood of violence than the general population. Undiagnosed and untreated, however, and the likelihood of adverse outcomes spikes. Additionally, add the variables of substance abuse or dependence, and the incidences of catastrophic outcomes becomes more and more of a possibility.

The safety pertaining to an individual's behavior who is ensconced in a state of psychotic madness is a most interesting and important consideration. I certainly can understand such a concern. Both traditionally and perhaps prima facie, the understanding of a psychotic individual likely is correlated with someone who may be violent. But for purposes of a meticulous clarity, it must foremost be understood that psychosis and violence are universally two and not one. Nevertheless, in a generalized consideration, is a madman a safe man? I believe the answer to this question to be nuanced and based on certain conditions. I think a psychotic individual experiencing such symptoms as auditory hallucinations, paranoia, and delusions is much more prone to safety issues during the time of the first initial onset of the illness and also in instances when the individual's thought disorder is untreated, undiagnosed, and/or is clinically unmediated. This is a generalization, but it is also a significant differentiation. Contrary to popular belief, and perhaps as a product of topical ignorance, those with mental illness are no more likely to engage in criminality than those of the general population. Of course, numbers can always be skewed for intended purposes but generally conceived the stigma regarding the connection of mental illness and criminality is largely a myth. Yes, some individuals with mental illness commit crimes but so too do the rest of the population. I do contend, however, that untreated mental illness is an altogether distinct categorization and of an entirely different consideration.

The treatment of mental illness goes well beyond simply administering medication. No doubt medications play a significant role at times in helping individuals, but medication is not treatment in its totality, at least not always. I consider "**psychoeducation**" paramount in the treatment process. Psychoeducation is the clinical term used to describe the process of education concerning one's mental illness. Psychoeducation refers to psychological education. Being informed about the symptoms of one's mental illness is conducive to enhanced coping and can be contributory to the overall recovery process. Of course, as with any type of education, there are varying levels of acumen. Some are more informed than others. Many individuals live with mental illness with limited knowledge about their affliction, while others are well-informed and quite knowledgeable. In the clinical realm of psychology, educating individuals about their mental illness is considered "**best practice**." Best practice is a term used to describe empirical, research tested and confirmed, statistically proven clinical methodology. In other words, if an individual goes to a mental health therapist for treatment, part of the content and process of therapy should include psychoeducation. If an individual with mental illness, therefore, engages in comprehensive treatment, including medication if deemed appropriate alongside talk-therapy services, that individual is no more likely to engage in criminality than those of the general population. I think this statement may be contrary to the generalized public belief, at least perhaps in part. Untreated mental illness, however, is of its own categorical subset and often can cause problems across many life realms, including possible criminal and legal entanglements. Now, given the differentiation of treated versus untreated mental illness, let us return to the pertinent question of "is a madman a safe man?"

What are the specified safety considerations in regard to those with schizo disorders? Firstly, in the clinical realms of psychiatry and psychology, safety issues are often categorically divided into the domains of "harm-to-self" and "harm-to-others." Harm-to-self often refers to issues with suicidality, although it certainly can also refer to other manners and methods of self-harm not of **suicidal intent**. Suicidality is a clinical term and it is used as a generalized descriptor that includes all potential variables associated with the presentation of an individual wanting to end one's life. Suicidality presents with a spectrum of clinical considerations including variables related to one's thoughts and also to one's behaviors. The concept of suicidality is often deconstructed into the clinical terms of suicidal "ideation," suicidal "gestures," and suicide "attempts." Ideation is the term used to describe having thoughts about the act of committing suicide. Ideation is then further grouped by the subtypes known as "intent" and "plan." Intent refers to an individual with active ideation and the present motivation to commit the act. Plan refers to methodology. Plans may include such exemplary methods as using a firearm, overdose, stepping into traffic, or by hanging as just a few of the many possible means.

Many individuals over the course of a lifetime, those with mental illness or not, may experience thoughts of suicide. And although perhaps not contributory to happiness and general well-being, suicidal thoughts are largely harmless. Thoughts are simply thoughts and do not have to have any corresponding action to them. **Suicidal gestures**, however, move on the spectrum of suicidality to becoming more of a danger to an individual. A suicidal gesture is a pseudo-suicidal act or behavior of self-harm with the associated global intent of a sustained self-preservation. Examples of suicidal gestures may include significantly cutting oneself but deliberately short of lethality or overdosing on pills but deliberately too few to suicide. These typified behaviors have the intent of self-harm but not of suicide. Such gestures often come with an associated suicidal veneer.

Suicide, of course, references a self-induced manner of death. The possible means of suicide attempts are many, and when such acts are committed with sufficient lethality completed suicide is the outcome. An act with dispositional intent without lethality differentiates to the outcome of a suicide attempt. From a clinical perspective, an individual with temporally active **suicidal ideation**, intent, and plan is considered the highest risk for suicide. All of variables of suicidality present under the clinical moniker of potential self-harm. By manner of profession, any issues of suicidality will always be met with a clinical deterrence.

Beyond the considerations associated with suicidality belies yet further differentiated categories under the clinical moniker of self-harm. These, too, can be dangerous to the self although not of lethal intent or outcome. An exemplary self-harm behavior is that of cutting oneself. Many individuals cut themselves intentionally without any intent to kill themselves. Eating disorders too can be a form of deliberate self-harm without the intent of suicidality. In a most general sense, mental illness and **harm-to-self** can have clinical correlates but certainly not at all times. Pertaining specifically to thought disorders, suicidality and acts of self-harm can both be clinical concerns depending on presenting symptomatology. Chronic self-harm behaviors, such as chronic cutting behaviors and issues with eating, usually fall under mental health diagnoses other than that of schizo disorders. Suicidality can present in schizo disorders, but issues with other types of self-harm behaviors usually fall under alternative diagnoses.

How, therefore, do individuals with schizo diagnoses reach the point of having issues with suicidality? My intent is not to cover the issues of safety in any totality but more in just a general sense and as easily and fundamentally understood. Therefore, how do schizo disorders and the issue of suicidality mesh? Simply put, when one is psychotic, one generally is maladjusted in several life realms, and consequently, one can oftentimes become quite **dysphoric**. In addition to feelings of dysphoria, one's perceptions can become radically opposed to the mutually agreed upon socially constructed reality of the masses. Therefore, dysphoric feelings, based in part on cognitive and perceptive distortions and inclusive of the issues of paranoia, delusions, and auditory hallucinations can lead to lethal actions. It is not uncommon for suicidality to present at some point in the presentation of a schizo disorder. Unfortunately, there are many outcomes of completed suicide although this is but a subset of the greater majority. The issue of suicidality, therefore, can be an important clinical consideration in the presentation of a schizo disorder especially over the lifetime course of the disorder. But in a most general sense, acts of deliberate self-harm not of suicidal intent usually present in diagnostics other than those of schizo disorders.

The second realm of consideration pertaining to safety issues in relation to mental illness, and particularly in those with schizo disorders, is the categorization of "**harm-to-others**." The general clinical moniker of harm-to-others belies on a spectrum inclusive to considerations pertaining to one's thoughts, behaviors, and outcomes. From a clinical perspective, harm-to-others can involve both emotional and physical harm. An example of emotional harm-to-others could be found in verbally abusive domestic relationships. Another example may be found in parental verbal abuse or parental neglect, that being, parents emotionally harming their child or neglecting the generalized well-being of the child. Harsh, insulting, and derogatory language towards a child is an example of emotional harm-to-others. Physical harm-to-others can include assaults, homicides, murders, rapes, and severe corporal punishment (of a child). The diagnostics, exclusive of thought disorders, that often present in individuals that engage in harm-to-others include **antisocial personality disorder, conduct disorders**, and **narcissistic personality disorder**. Personality disorders often apply to individuals that engage in repeated abusive behavior. Single incidences of violence, contrarily, do not usually necessitate a personality disorder. But, returning to point, that being the connection of schizo disorders and harm-to-others, there are salient reasons for an individual with a thought disorder to engage in harm-to-others. Persecutory delusional thought content can cause an individual to act out and engage in harm-to-others. Auditory hallucinations can also be contributory to violent acts, especially **command auditory hallucinations** that direct an individual to commit harm-to-others. Command auditory hallucinations are hallucinogenic voices that command or tell the symptomatic individual to commit particular behaviors. In a general manner, therefore, a psychotic state with all of its possible inherent variables can be facilitative to an individual causing harm-to-others but certainly not necessarily so. Those with a thought disorder are more likely to engage in single acts of harm-to-others rather than a pattern of such behavior. And to reiterate, found patterns of violence are usually more indicative of issues with a personality disorder.

The last consideration pertaining to harm-to-others in the context of a thought disorder is that of the "criminally insane." Certainly, the legal terminology of "innocent by reason of insanity" is generally a well-known legal status and state of affairs. When this phrase is used it is almost assuredly in reference to an individual with recent psychosis or with a presenting schizo disorder. Again, psychosis is a conglomerate of symptoms that causes an individual to disconnect with the mutually shared socially constructed reality. Other than the diagnostics of schizo disorders, psychosis can also occur in individuals with bipolar disorder, severe depression, dissociative disorders, and certain neurocognitive disorders (referenced as dementia). When one commits an act of violence while in an active psychotic state, the courts therefore have quite the conundrum. The question becomes the following: Are individuals in a psychotic state due to mental illness responsible for their actions? I am not a lawyer and I have not worked in the legal system, but I would suspect this state of affairs can be quite the muddled legal abyss. Thought disorders and issues with psychosis are tightly enmeshed, and psychosis is not an affliction of any personal choosing. It is an involuntary imposition. Therefore, are individuals in an involuntary symptomatic psychotic state necessarily responsible for their actions?

Based on my personal experience, allow me to explain my thoughts on the matter of personal responsibility of one's actions while psychotic. Firstly, any violent behavior that would have been of possibility on my part would have been far more likely to occur during the initial onset of psychosis. Why would this be so? As one may intuit, while experiencing a first onset of psychosis, this is the time of the illness when behavior is likely to be most erratic and unpredictable. During my first onset of psychosis, I had no understanding that I was having symptoms indicative of a mental illness, let alone any issues with psychosis. Any potential insight was altogether absent, and I had a complete lack of any knowledge of any possible underlying condition. Psychosis and ignorance is a potential volatile combination with possible life-altering consequences. Symptoms such as persecutory delusions and command hallucinations can impel an individual to commit violent acts that otherwise would not be inherent in their person. During this time frame of the first onset of psychosis, unfortunately for many, one-time acts of violence can have life-altering consequences for both the perpetrator and certainly the victim. Such a violent act may have never been possible for the same individuals absent of their unchosen psychosis. These outcomes are tragedies all around. Additionally, determining any legal culpability, I can well imagine, would be quite the legal quandary. In my experience, during my first onset of psychosis, I most certainly engaged in many erratic behaviors and verbiages that when absent of psychosis I would have never considered yet alone acted upon. My psychotic states produced behavior non-germane to my rational personality. In my particular instance, my non-normative social behaviors and verbiages did not cross into the realm of violent acts, although admittedly I was most fortunate in this sense. But certainly, I was most erratic at the time of the initial onset particularly due to the absence of any insight.

To this very day and until tomorrow, I will continue to refine my prevailing insight regarding all things psychosis and of its related cognitive distortions. For you see, my dear reader, insight is an altogether open-ended process. There is no endpoint to this cognitive task. For only by course of insight does gainful sustenance follow. Learning how to manage my behavior while cognitively psychotic is a skill singularly panned from decades of hard-earned insight. Only from insight have I learned to be acutely aware to monitor my words and my behaviors when I am psychotic to ensure I behave in a most rational manner. When coping with my disorder, I am now so highly cognizant of my symptoms that I would no longer consider myself a candidate to engage in any kind of violence. However, this is the state of the current affairs as opposed to the time of first onset. During the first onset of psychosis, I certainly engaged in behavior that otherwise would be absent. This leads me to conclude that other individuals, when psychotic, also may engage in behaviors that otherwise would be absent, especially during the early stages of the illness. Admittedly and unfortunately, I can certainly understand an individual committing a violent act secondary to issues with a presenting psychosis. In my case, I was fortunate enough to escape any life-altering acts with potential tragic consequences. Others are not so lucky.

I can infer from my own experience that issues with psychosis can have potential safety ramifications, especially and particularly when insight is low or otherwise absent. As far as safety issues, I contend insight is a most powerful and protective elixir. Nevertheless, in regard to safety issues, again, "There but for the grace of God go I." Acts of violence both to self and others, are the poorest of outcomes and are often tragedies on all accounts. Psychosis can certainly lead to such acts and unfortunately this is simple fact. But when considering the moral imperatives behind such acts, ambiguity prevails. The issue of whether one is personally responsible for their actions while actively psychotic becomes an issue heaped in delineations and produces complex legal, clinical, and moral distinctions and conclusions. In my instance, at this point in my illness some twenty plus years past initial onset, I should be held to the normative standards of moral imperative. My thinking may be besieged by psychosis, but, nevertheless, I have capacity for behavioral responsibility, at least in terms of acts of legality. Even so, I must admit that not all with psychosis will be in concert with my trajectory. So enters the muddled quagmire of judgmental distinctions. Beyond all this dubiousness, however, I can definitively offer that during the time of the first onset of my psychosis, such adverse outcomes were of an exponentially higher likelihood. My presenting lack of insight gave me no reign over my behaviors and conduct. Therefore, generalizing my experience to that of others, it leads me to definitively conclude that psychosis, given certain conditions, can definitively promulgate potential safety issues. I believe this to be an unfortunate fact with disheartening consequences. As far a responsibility for one's actions while psychotic and in favor of a moral conclusion, I find this a complex issue and to be best parsed on a specified basis. An applicable universal or generalized conclusion simply does not pertain. Rather, such instances must be discriminated specifically and by manner of each act unto its own. As such, in consideration and judgment of any such acts and an associated culpability, together we must necessarily wade in an ambiguous and ubiquitous moral quagmire.

10

Despite Psychosis, the Sun Rises Yet Again

How then does one live effectively when having a psychotic disorder? To address this question, I would like to explore the concept of "insight" and how it pertains to my experience of mental illness and, in particular, in relation to paranoid schizophrenia. Without any hesitation or doubt, I assert that insight is my paramount protective factor in managing my thought disorder. Insight is the accumulated knowledge over time concerning the totality of my mental illness. The term insight goes beyond the vernacular and in my usage is better understood in a clinical sense. The concept of insight, in relation to mental illness and in a clinical context, can have profound meaning and significant implications. In my experience, insight has developed over time both incrementally and cumulatively. In living with such a haphazard illness, insight has become my control variable. It avails cognitive allowances subject to my whimsies and manipulations, and its sequelae provides for my consistent psychological assuagement. In a most basic manner, insight is analogous to the adage of knowing the "tricks of the trade." I dare say without insight into my illness, I would be persistently psychotic, highly erratic, and mostly miserable. Insight is my intellectual understanding of my specified schizophrenia. Along its temporal course, I have learned many lessons in its management. I suppose in this sense it runs parallel with the rest of life in its inherent lessons learned from trial and error. And make no mistake, along the way there have been lessons aplenty. During the time of the initial onset of my psychosis, my insight was altogether absent, and I was ignorant. I was highly symptomatic from my disorder and I had no inkling whatsoever that I was experiencing symptoms of a mental illness. Such a conclusion never crossed my mind. During the first onset of my psychosis I did sense a shifting from my usual experiences, but I attributed it to other possible etiologies, including a developmental rationalization of transitioning out of academia and into the "real world." Although my experiences were in stark contrast from my known and felt experiential history, I would have had better odds at winning the Powerball lottery than concluding I was mentally ill with schizophrenia. I was in complete and total ignorance. I had no reference points. Mental illness did not present in my family lineage and it was unknown to me through any auxiliary relationships. Therefore, upon my descent into madness during the time of the first onset of psychosis, why would I attribute my experiences to a mental illness? There was no knowledge base to make such an inferential discernment.

There are innumerable afflictions that present across the human condition. Afflictions for which there are no volunteers. Afflictions that court no suitors. For some, however, afflictions can largely be dodged at least that is for a significant portion of one's life. Such fortunate individuals may have met all developmental milestones, are largely healthy without disease or malady, come from good families, and are generally well-adjusted in adulthood. These individuals, as adults, may have good jobs with ample income, and may live the dream of house, family, career, and children. I label this phenomenon the "charmed-life theory" and I am always enchanted by its presence. Some may live decades without significant hardship. I find such fortunate outcomes most intriguing. For those of charmed lives, affliction may steadfastly procrastinate in its presence. It seems to me, however, that eventually all of humanity succumbs. It is just a matter of timing. For some it may sooner and for some it may later. But for all, I find it inevitable.

In my experience, the charmed-life ended in my early teens when my father, whom I dearly loved, passed away from a brutal and persistent brain cancer. The charmed-life further eroded with the occurrence of my mental illness in my early twenties. Following these experiences, and upon further contemplation, I have come to understand that affliction is parcel to the human condition. The mere presence of a looming death, shrouded in all its mystery, joins all of humanity in a common dilemma and affliction. Certainly, afflictions can vary greatly in degree and severity and this is of an utmost consequence. The well-worn adage of "life isn't fair" aptly applies here as a most appropriate truism. And for some unknown reason, suffering is not equitable in Its distribution, and its supply is a seemingly endless fountainhead entirely absent of any singular human demand. Additionally, the multitudes of afflictions seem to present without end, including both the more common to the more novel. At all times suffering abounds. Just look to the news on any given day and one will read about an affliction that occurred to our brethren. The permutations are unceasing. Affliction becomes parcel to the human condition, inclusive to all, at least at some point over the course of one's life. Some escape affliction for significant periods of time, others are not so fortunate. Of course, eventually, we all must "die." The universal phenomenon of death ultimately unifies the human family, at least to some degree. The spectrum and variable presentations of affliction never ceases to amaze. I feel my affliction, in the totality of human possibilities, is a rather benign affliction to manage in comparison to other brutal and disabling possibilities. I am humbled I do not have to manage a more intense malady.

As I began to describe, insight into my mental illness was entirely absent during the first onset of psychosis. Why was this so? I suppose it is a bit like life in general in that there are learning curves to many aspects of our existence. We try not to make the same mistake twice and we try to learn from errors so that in the future we will be better-suited. And so like any subject matter, the issues pertaining to mental illness also came with a learning curve. My learning curve began at the first onset of psychosis. I started at ignorance and over the years, after many a dark tribulation, a recognizance developed, and an intangible characteristic was forged. Schizophrenia tested my will and it almost became like I had a singular choice between a broken spirit or alternatively a rebellious integrity. And after ample doses of disturbing emotional turmoil, a psychological tipping point emerged. I reached a point in this illness when I knew I had won the war. I also knew that all the subsequent battles would not always end in my favor. But I knew I had won. I had reached a most visceral conclusion and I achieved a psychological resolution. I had concluded that whatever schizophrenia proffered that in the end I would maintain my psychological integrity and a capable level of social and emotional functioning. I even knew I may be hospitalized once again, but it no longer mattered. I knew that given time I would always recover in my emotional-cognitive capacities. Acuity no longer ruled, as I began to understand the bigger picture of life. For you see my dear reader, I have discovered the daily battles of life do not always go in your favor, but if you can take the wider and more accurate viewpoint of life, then the daily details become less and less significant and the life total becomes much clearer. Life takes clarity from tribulation because it points one directly toward priorities. And once priorities are recognized and appreciated, the war is won and the battles become less significant. I knew that certain limitations in my life may be a consequence of this illness but at the same time I also knew I had the resolve to persist and to do so with both clarity and purpose. In a most odd manner, schizophrenia taught me my priorities. Of this, I call insight.

Insight facilitates my coping, my healing, and especially my assuagement. Mental illness lends to periods of remission, but a cure is most generally absent. Insight into my mental illness consists of the sum of my psychotic experiences denominated by its lessons, themes, recurrent patterns, similarities, and differences. Delusional thought content I had two months ago, similar to content of delusions I had five to ten years ago, does not have the power it once did. The delusion becomes more familiar and less intimidating. Familiar delusions lend themselves to the adage "I have been through this before." This attitude helps in my ability to cope, at least at times and in part. Familiarity is not curative, but it certainly is helpful.

Insight present or insight lacking, I maintain that at times certain symptoms can still be causal to a terrifying existence. Persecutory delusions, for example, frequently trigger perceived dire existential determinations. For example, a personal recurrent persecutory delusion of mine holds the belief that of all humanity, including family and those considered friends, hate me and want me to suffer. This is a most disturbing delusion. This delusion also includes the thought content that God also hates me and wants me to suffer. The interpersonal consequences of these enmeshed delusional beliefs make functioning, including in the workplace, a most challenging situation. How does one converse with others with such underlying thought content along with its corresponding feelings of hurt, aloneness, isolation, and hopelessness? The experience is of a total existential abandonment and the feelings are acutely persecutory. Additionally, when I have such delusions, the situation is believed to be my personal static existential truth. Feelings of absolute hopelessness enter along with terrifying existential conclusions. This delusion is very difficult to manage, especially when it is thought of in the terms of an unrelenting reality and an underlying personal truth. Ultimately, however, given some time, the ideation slowly dismantles from its whole and reduces into nonsensical impotent pieces and fragments. Then, it is gone altogether. So although insight is certainly important and most helpful, it is not a panacea. But because of the elixir of insight, I have learned the importance of holding on for just one more minute, one more hour, or for just one more day, and then hopefully with time such delusions will ultimately come to pass.

Over the years, I have learned much about my illness and the protective factor of insight certainly is extremely helpful. Early in my illness, when experiencing symptoms, my behavior and conversations would be highly erratic, irrational, and often inappropriate to context. A most important coping skill I have developed over time as a result of improved insight is the vital importance of monitoring my own behaviors and conversations. When symptomatic, I am fastidiously diligent in remaining as rational and appropriate as I am innately capable despite having thought content that is highly conducive to acting out in maladaptive, erratic, and irrational manners. A current episode of psychosis could have the same or similar thought content as an episode many years back, including during the first onset. But although the content is similar, my behaviors and conversations are now vastly different. I no longer act out in the manner I once did. Due to improved insight, I may have the same thought content as yesteryear but now with different behaviors. That is the power of insight. Now, when I am psychotic, I self-monitor myself to remain as rational, logical, normative, and unobtrusive as possible. Initially, I had no such capacity and it led to erratic behavior and multiple psychiatric hospitalizations. I certainly do not want that type of outcome for myself. Therefore, now when actively symptomatic, I self-monitor to avoid all types of detrimental outcomes, including hospitalizations, loss of employment, and personal estrangements. Additionally, I also want to avoid unwanted attention from others regarding my behavior. In other words, when behaving in erratic manners secondary to psychosis, it then often becomes a very difficult enterprise to rationalize my inappropriate behaviors to others from a post-mortem context. It is often difficult to explain to others a narrative about my erratic behavior that they may buy as a legitimate explanation for my otherwise psychotic behavior. During the earlier times of my illness, I had been in this situation many times trying to explain to others why I acted as I did. In truth, I acted as I did because I was psychotic, but others certainly did not know this to be the cause. In these delicate past situations, I well knew I acted erratically because I was psychotic. The reasoning was no mystery to me. Sometimes my contrived rationalizations for my behavior carried persuasion and other times not so much. In a sense, I was trying to discount my psychotic behavior post-mortem by course of some fabricated narrative that carried rational explanation regarding my irrational behavior. I rationalized to others for reasons of personal sustenance. I tried to cover for my mental illness.

Psychosis can put priorities in order fast. Jobs and money are priorities, and I certainly get that, but here is my personal advice to any who may care. Guess what? Even after job reprimand or even being fired, life continues much like the waves of the ocean undeterred. The sun rises and sets again. Breath enters and exits the lungs again. The birds chirp despite your perceived crisis. Please do not misconstrue. I want to do well in employment and it is important and needed, but if it doesn't work out, it just doesn't work out. The sun rises yet again. Over time, I have realized that life and work are distinct. Life will indifferently plod along regardless of job status. For most, work becomes a priority and many significantly stress themselves regarding aspects of their job. In a sense, life becomes strictly parts and the healthy whole recedes. Personal experience becomes fractured into the pieces of work life versus home life, and this terse dichotomy becomes the existential whole. Because of schizophrenia, I have endured enough vocational "failures" to last me tenfold. But I have realized a few pertinent things. Firstly, life is much richer than the either/or paradigm of work versus home life. Do not subjugate your life into this either/or, Jack-in-the-Box paradigm. Jack-in-the-Box pops up, Jack is home feeling free and happy. With his arrival at work, Jack descends below now feeling confined and unhappy. But I proffer, this is not the transcendental whole. After all, it's just a job. The sun will rise again. Life is too textured to be shoved into the either/or paradigm of work life versus home life. Stop and smell the roses so to speak. Root, root, root for the home team. Create something that takes time and patience. Watch the sunset for no good reason. Just try not to violently separate your life into work versus home. In the end, it may just be a giant waste of time and energy. Due to my mental illness, including issues with psychosis, my priorities have certainly shifted. I still work and want to work, but it is only a small fraction of the totality of life. And if it doesn't work out, miraculously, and with its enduring ease, the sun rises yet again, so do not worry.

Over the course of many years, every so often and on occasion, my schizophrenia has been directly causal to patently absurd and utterly ridiculous thought content. When of this typified characteristic, in a certain manner, it has now lent itself to some perceived personal amusement. Certainly, initially it did not. The first onset of psychosis was evil and disturbing. In the early years of the illness, it was bereft of any amusement or humor. Some twenty years later, though, it is a different tale, at least in part. In a general sense, my symptoms are never welcome visitors and in no manner are they enjoyable when in their midst. So when I assert some amusement, it is to be understood as on an occasional basis, and under specific conditions and circumstances. Nevertheless, why such a timbre? I think it is mostly because of the absolute ridiculousness of my thought content at times as combined with its consequential absurd predications. Sometimes, while psychotic, my perceptions are unfathomable. These typical perceptions would be otherwise unconjurable by my asymptomatic mind. My psychosis often sullies the boundary of existential possibility. For example, I've had recurrent psychotic experiences when I feel I am literally speaking with God. I do not mean in an exaggerated figurative sense, but succinctly in a literal manner. In my perceptions, God has incarnated Himself into human form, and there I stand in conversation with the Almighty. Personal experiences such as these obliterate the established boundaries of my sane mind and introduce perceptions and thought content that is truly surreal by nature. As such, at times I dreamily reflect about these most novel experiences and approach a state of wonderment and astonishment and on the very best of days it will tickle my mind ever so gently with tinges of amusement. Then I wonder yet again about metaphysical truthfulness.

Just as a reiteration, I have had only a few positive psychotic experiences. Such positive experiences I could likely count on one hand. Almost entirely, psychotic experiences are very difficult, unwanted, disturbing, and often debilitating. But on the rare occasion, the script flips and the doom and gloom miraculously becomes the polar opposite and all things bad turn to all things good. These experiences are very few and when they do occur, they are brief (usually under an hour). Nevertheless, at times, when a psychotic experience somehow transmutes from all negative to all positive, it can be an illuminating experience. One positive psychotic experience I had was an episode in my late twenties about five years into the illness. I found myself in a perceived literal dialogue with God, not aloud but in my mind, and I perceived the dialogue as real. I had no doubts about the experience. I was immersed in the belief. It was not a prayerful monologue but rather a one-to-one conversational communion. The boundaries of my thought content were pushed so far out of the normative and the rational that I believed, without any doubt or reservation, that I was in fact conversing with God. Pertaining to this claim, I would wager that most would deny it as a likelihood or even as a possibility. Many would discount it as simply the conjuring of a nutcase. I, too, can discount it as just a stressed and tired psychotic state of mind ripe with auditory hallucinations. But even to this day, the experience lingers in my mind with an indubitable veracity. Now, I should temper this with the fact that psychotic disorders are well-known to provoke **religious ideation**. It is a common delusional presentation. Nevertheless, this specified religious experience, delusional or not, to this day maintains a stirring psychological profundity. And this is yet another example of the paradox of schizophrenia. The experience presents with the utmost of veracity, but for my own mental health I must deny my perceptual indications.

To cope with such typical psychotic paradoxes, I live on a slivered fence that ever so vaguely delineates "that which is and that which is not." Of such typical vaguers, I have made my metaphysical peace and I have found sturdy posture. This particular religious experience was too real to discount in total as solely the product of psychosis. But, at that time, I was indeed psychotic. Nevertheless, for whatever reason, a spiritual God-based ideation emerged void of persecutory content (as is the norm) and it was an altogether positive albeit brief experience. This type of positive experience in individuals with psychosis is not entirely foreign. Some have regular positive experiences, amid the otherwise sinister, and I too have had a handful. The great majority of my experiences, however, remain ever dark and by ratio cast an ample shadow on the positive. But I find such deleterious quantifications to lack a personal difference for I am certain life and mathematics are two and not one. Further, I find no redeeming value in a substantive selective abstraction from the psychotic whole. I have learned to avoid personal metaphysical conclusions based on knee-jerk reactions to my clandestine psychosis. Rather, I simply construct my life perspectives of a personal choosing and of an intentional construction and I cast experiential ratios aside. And by this manner, the paradox of psychosis recedes once more and consequently my ever-abiding hope floweth restorative but now yet twofold.

So on this most particular of days, I began dialoguing with God in a most assured and indubitable manner. And what was the content of our "conversation?" Well, initially I was praying to God for mercy. I felt so entirely persecuted by the world that my only perceived salvation during this time of hopelessness and darkness was an appeal to God. Then, while I was occupied in prayer and petition and from the eye of my contemplation, God spoke. And upon word one, my despair was abruptly vanquished then followed by the further miraculous. Light permeated my being. A sublimity filled the depths of my pores. God then explained to me in such clarity and with such love about why in fact I felt the way I did. God explained to me my suffering and it made complete sense. God explained to me that historically others too have been persecuted but that in his wisdom it had purpose and meaning and that it was benevolent. At this point, I felt tremendous relief and peace, but the experience did not end there.

The conversation with God continued over the course of the next few minutes. After God explained to me the why's of my suffering, what followed was nothing less than astonishing. God told me he was going to, and I quote as verbatim from God, "show me heaven on Earth." The words bolted through my psychology and did so with a sterling sense of love, power, and voraciousness. Then, the next fifteen minutes were unquestionably the most sublime moments of my entire life. After God spoke, my yet prone position quickly became passé and an urgency ensued to head outdoors. Amid the warm summer air, the conversation continued. God was intimately with me in my thoughts. As I walked, God taught. He explained my suffering so I could understand. He explained nature and creation. The experiential sublimity was overwhelming. My heart, mind, and soul felt warm and peaceful, far beyond any compare, and an alluring yellowish hue took to my eyes sighted. Then, things suddenly turned humorous. God joked, and it was all too funny. I ultimately made it to my destination, that being the pizza shop, and I grabbed a slice and sat at the booth. Then, after a few more humorous comments by God, the experience abruptly ended. It felt like a abundant power bolted to exits of my mind. And just like that, it was over. I was once again left to my own devices, but now traced with an experiential longing. Over the course of my illness, I have had repeated ideations regarding God, and as previously stated, it is not uncommon for individuals with thought disorders to have such ideations. Spiritual themes are common. In my instance, such religiosity routinely comes accompanied by fear. But on a handful of occasions has come the sublime. So, I ask you, would like personal experiences carry any relevance to your life or would you simply nay say? As for me, a derivative but yet unbeaten path has been laid forthright and I know of its destination. But more on destiny a bit later, my dear reader, for psychosis fully descript still yet beckons.

Psychosis leans on the boundaries of my thought. When I am asymptomatic, my thought content is much more normative, utilitarian, and neutral. When psychosis emerges, however, I find myself thinking about possibilities and scenarios far outside of my normalized thought. Additionally, psychosis is characteristically emotionally intense compared to my leveled asymptomatic thought. Normalized thought is much like a pedestrian stroll. Psychosis is like holding on for dear life at the end of an ignited rocket ship. It can be intensely disturbing and always is a most unwelcome intruder. Oftentimes, when immersed in psychotic thought, my perceptions are earnestly distorted and consequently my experiences become brutal to endure. With my psychosis comes paranoia, hopelessness, and oft feelings of eternal damnation. When I am psychotic, I feel trapped in a punitive labyrinth with no availing Tao for escape. There simply is "**No Exit.**" During these times, I really do hate it.

Psychotic thought is disturbing. It serves a cold dish of hopelessness and damnation. It comes parcel with feelings of inescapability. But on a few rare occasions, and perhaps it is when I am feeling particularly resilient and rebellious, psychotic thought content can present as so thoroughly adverse that the whole ideational conglomerate collapses into a feeling of absolute and total ridiculousness. This "collapse" phenomenon occurs at a most macro level. Delusions are only delusions because they are believable. Remember, a delusion is simply a term for a "false belief." Therefore, when a delusion loses its believability, the content collapses into metaphysical nonsense. This usually occurs due to the emergence of an alternative perspective or possibility. When a new way of looking at things arrives, the delusion loses its persuasion. Delusions have weaknesses and vulnerabilities just like everything else under the sun. And when they dissipate due to incoherence, I then return to sanity for a donut and a coffee. Oftentimes, my delusions assertively plant me into very unusual existential predicaments. The spell and mysticism of a delusion can create an existential context nothing less than utterly ridiculous and bizarrely absurd. But eureka! I have discovered that oftentimes just one very small step and just a few very small moments beyond my ridiculous and bizarre psychological cohorts comes the phenomenon of psychotic ideational collapse followed by feelings of a most sweet temporal relief. I love when psychotic content collapses. It is much akin to the detonation of a most faulty structure. Whirling clouds of dust appear as the once entrenched structure succumbs to its fate of collapse and obliteration. Once the destruction is complete, my psychological victory is claimed and in moment of inspiration a Tao again emerges, and I once again see a path of safe escape. With relief and ease I shoulder on but most of my victories are short-lived. Inevitably the delusions begin anew, and the cycle recurs. But such it is. I no longer try to change the spots inherent to the leopard. I face yet another day in the inclement jungle. But no matter, for over the years I have built a safe haven and I call this dwelling insight. So I take another small step forward and remain ever yet steadfast and undeterred.

The specious moments following the collapse of delusional content is often accompanied by a now familiar experience. It takes the feeling of being on the receiving end of a practical joke. The joke, that being the delusional ideation, comes to an end in a sometimes-comical manner. "Alright," I will say to myself after emerging from the damned perceptions, "The joke's over, I get it." The delusional content dissipates, and I enjoy a few moments of comic relief. And when I have time away from social activity and in the solitude of my own space, I often retrospect about my recent psychotic experiences. The experiences are at times so surreal that when reflecting post-mortem, I oftentimes feel compelled to guffaw. "Too bizarre to be true," I will think and laugh. With the passing oftentimes comes the reflective humor.

I like to call my psychotic experiences "episodes." I find my psychotic experiences analogous in many ways to a TV program. My psychotic experiences often initiate with a type of thematic introduction, followed by the body of the delusional content, and with conclusion upon ideational collapse. In my self-talk when I use the term episode, I am doing so in an exasperated yet comical framing. These repeated experiences are so crazy, crazy, and crazy, that once passed I can only shake my head in utter disbelief accompanied by a most subtle Mona Lisa smile. Similarly to TV, when one episode ends the next soon begins. With a new psychotic episode comes a new plot with unexpected twists performed among new actors (my dear reader, I must inform you I make slight of psychosis intentionally; I try to maintain an attitude of rebellion mixed with an apoplectic sense of humor; I have found this disposition to be highly protective to my remaining sanity; But it is no matter, for it is the end that matters and not so much the steps along the way).

I often think my psychotic experiences are the physical equivalent of being repeatedly slammed into a wall. As my psychotic ideas present over time, I feel like my mind is being slammed against the wall hit after hit after hit. It is often experientially exhausting. The consequences of eternal damnation, after all, have very significant ramifications. Feeling eternally damned is not an experience easily brushed off and simply forgotten. It is serious business, at least when amid the delusional experience. But I always remind myself to be patient with allowance for time curative. And heretofore, with a mandatory knock on a most sturdy oak, all such typical psychotic episodes have eventually come to pass with an associated temporal fade into my time-ago gestalt. And with each psychotic passing, the thunderhead again obliges the sun, and to its light returns my psychological inclination.

11

My Most Excellent Elixir!

Living with psychosis for many years with multitudes of adverse experiences eventually has led to so-called insight into my illness. Insight is the clinical term used for the improving knowledge and coping abilities in relation to one's mental illness. I previously began writing about insight, but then made a felt tangent in lieu of an overly dull literary mechanism. And with said tangent comes a renewed vigor and energy to more thoroughly develop the theme of insight. For insight, my dear reader, is my most excellent elixir!

In my instance, the growth of my insight over the course and time of the illness has led to improvements in my coping abilities and consequently in my outcomes. It is with the utmost of certitude that I assert insight as the principal factor in effectively managing my schizophrenia. When you first learn how to ride a bike, fall off, and sustain an abrasion, at this point insight begins to develop in regard to safety on a bike. It is the same with mental illness. In the beginning, I was repeatedly falling off the bike due to inexperience. But over time and through trial and error, I learned and became more capable. This is an exemplary microcosm to life in general. We all learn from our past to be better-suited for our future. With experience comes insight.

During the first onset of psychosis, my insight was a robust zero on the prevailing spectrum. I had no experience or exposure to issues with mental illness leading up to the time of the first onset. Schizophrenia descended on my mind and my thoughts with no clarifying declaration to its arrival. As I previously discussed, during the time of the first onset of psychosis, things were changing in my life and things began to seem different from my normative experience. Making the inferential leap, however, that I was experiencing psychosis was an absolute zero probability. Additionally, my familial supports too had no inkling of any such possibility.

Understanding the dynamics regarding the first onset is a critical aspect to conquering schizophrenia. With the first onset of psychosis routinely comes erratic behavior. The erratic behavior will present chronologically over time and in various social contexts. During this initial stage, an individual's level of functioning can drastically decline. Most who experience a first onset will have no prior education about the complexities of schizophrenia. During the first onset of psychosis, the illness attacks its target with an initial subtlety and in a most obstructed manner. It begins as a sneak attack but culminates in a bludgeon. Because of a lack of insight, with no-to-little understanding of the illness, the first onset of psychosis oftentimes is the most disruptive phase of the illness. A lack of insight becomes the antecedent to consequent erratic behavior. It is a most terse logical equation. At times, the outcomes can be drastic and life-altering. Such poor outcomes may include hospitalization, legal entanglements, incarceration, family estrangement, social isolation, and harm-to-self or others. I dread for those who do not survive instigate psychosis yet unscathed from life-altering consequences. I was lucky. I count my blessings. Others wallow and I earnestly empathize.

Now with my therapist beret rightly affixed and adorned, my dear reader, let us explore some salient points from a professional and clinical perspective. There is new evidence-based data that indicates when individuals get involved in treatment during the temporal period known as the "first onset of psychosis" that the outcomes can take significantly improved trajectories compared to those that do not become linked to treatment. This recent clinical conclusion is based on repeated longitudinal studies. If an individual gets involved in treatment near to the first onset of psychosis it has been shown that the poor outcomes oftentimes can be significantly ameliorated. Clinical intervention at the first onset of psychosis is considered facilitative to improved outcomes and early intervention treatment is clinically on its way to "best practice." Best practice is a clinical term used to indicate the best treatment modalities for specified diagnoses. Best practice is the clinical gold standard. Best practice only becomes best practice after the approach, or the specified clinical intervention, has been research-tested and verified. With early intervention in regard to thought disorders, the poor outcomes can oftentimes fall in favor of more positive outcomes. The positive outcomes include such markers as continued high school and/or college attendance, continued employment or vocational pursuits, improved family relations, reduction in social isolation, and most importantly the reduction in potential life-altering negative consequences. Included in treatment during the first onset of psychosis is the modality or approach of "psychoeducation." Psychoeducation is the process of teaching those involved in treatment about what is known about the illness and what is known to be helpful. Psychoeducation will broach such topics as symptoms, medications, biology, temporal course, and generalized prognostics. Additionally, psychoeducation intends beyond the individual to the associated social support system, and by like manner and kind.

Interestingly, even as early as twenty years ago, the expected outcomes of schizophrenia were understood to be that of a great reduction in an individual's ability to function, including educationally, vocationally, and socially. During this era, the clinical message to the individual and their family, although well-intentioned, entailed inability, void ability. Work, if fathomable, would be "unskilled;" education, a non sequitur (the term "unskilled" labor I use as a moniker to convey the idea, although I feel the linguistic to be a poor semiotic. We all have skills, irregardless of pompous vocational stratification). And the further one delves into the history of mental illness, especially in consideration of those with thought disorders, the more abysmal the predicate and predication. The historical clinical perspective on thought disorders largely involved removing said individuals from the mainstream of society. Removal from the workplace, educational settings, and social contexts were the professional directives. Schizophrenics were thought incapable.

In my own experience, my first onset of psychosis was over 20 years ago, around 1993 to 1995. I lived with untreated psychosis for quite some time but when I eventually acquiesced to the necessity of routine and consistent treatment, circa 1996, it came by form and manner of **continuing day treatment** (jargonized as CDT), Now decades removed, I yet so clearly remember the moments just beyond my first steps in the door. My initiation included an introductory meeting with my designated therapist. During our initial come to pass, she provided me an item of info I found to be both equitably astounding and impertinent. My counsel included the unlikelihood of any future employment. She tagged this prognostic, however, with the possibility of a clinical exception. If ever so graced by an ample good fortune, such an anomaly would entail my capacity to someday "bag groceries" or the like. I have never forgotten this conversation and it is still motivating to this day. My eyes nearly fell from my face. I remember thinking "no, not me, I need to work, I have things to accomplish." I was resistant to old-school thought from the start. I had plans and aspirations, and schizophrenia carried no personal deterrence. My psychiatrist at the time, when speaking privately with my mother, reiterated the "bagging groceries" tagline also with the associated requisites of good fortune and ample time (and again, bagging groceries, in my opinion, is just as important and gainful as say the lawyer, or the accountant. I suppose I am too aware to stratify people in society according to their vocation; I prefer stratification based on a love quotient rather the dollar, but this is another matter altogether, so I digress!). My mother only told me of the comment many years later. She kept it tidily private because she did not want to impose on me any such limitations. She told me she went home after being told and cried. She was saddened by the message, especially coming from the expert on such matters. Anyway, just a mere twenty years ago the message was no work, no school, little socialization, and limited and diminished functioning. I was sold the bill of sales to take a permanent seat on the sideline of life. And the further in the past one looks as to the descript prognostics for schizophrenia, the more abysmal the findings, however well-intentioned. The modern conceptualization, however, is vastly different. The modern clinical perspective entails that schizophrenia is like any other disability, malady, or obstacle. The message is no longer "welcome to the sideline of life" but is now one of hope, normalization, functional capability, and productivity. And I do attest, it's an idea whose time has certainly come!

The current clinical message to individuals with mental illness largely involves the message of recovery and health. It includes work (no vocation exempt), education, social integration, and capacity for achievement similarly to the rest of the populous. Competent therapists will convey this message to the individual and family. The message is normative. The message conveys a health condition that properly attended to can be remedied and overcome similarly to the rest and any. No longer is the message I euphemistically reference as "welcome to the sideline of life." This message is now considered antiquated and most properly so. All goals remain viable. Sometimes, additional supports in vocational (i.e. job coach) or educational settings may assist, while at other times of no abiding requisite. The old message was of limits and poor prognostics. The new message entails capacity and achievement. There has been a radical shift away from a clinical deficit-model to a more strengths-based model. It has been a long time for the field to reach this point, but its declaration has arrived and it resounds in stripes. Modernity necessarily follows on the backs of pioneers and tipping points. I am always grateful for prior advocacies productive of current luxuries. The revolutionary perspective of abject capacity despite mental illness hallmarks in ranks as an emergent social justice. I am always most grateful and cognizant of the efforts of those before. From the bend of their backs, I can sip my wine. This I lest forget!

My dear reader, thank you for staying by my side through yet another most needed tangent. As you know, literary mechanism and I pair as a most uncomfortable cohort. Terse linearity is most characteristic of mathematics and logic and this is no such endeavor. But the time is now for digression and a return to theme for I no longer can allow to pass the operative methodology behind a prevailing psychological insight. So, by manner of accord and common gate, my dear reader, let us in return to trail and renew the grail of our ultimate literary destiny!.

12

Away from the Problem and Towards the Solution

My personal insight into my schizophrenia is based on an accumulated and ever-evolving understanding of the presentations of my mental illness. As I have previously explained, at the first onset of psychosis my insight was nil, and this is often the case for others as well. From the point of the first onset of psychosis until the current time, I have twenty-plus years of accumulated understanding. And frankly, it has been quite the treacherous journey. The psychological terrain of schizophrenia is perilous and can be full of potential pitfalls. But fear not, my dear reader, for the path laid implies destination, and destination we shall reach. For stardust is only the remains for the truly persistent.

Schizophrenia is tricky because it is not static. Via mutation and novelty, it relentlessly recreates. Its inherent constitution includes variables yet unknown and, as such, comes absent of any guarantees. But no matter, as it is not guarantees I seek. Rather, I search for hope and a viable psychological path. Insight manages but it does not cure. And at times, psychosis can trump insight, especially specious experiences not yet subject to the faculty of introspection by course of retrospection. Psychosis certainly can win some of its wagered battles, but I assure you, my dear reader, that insight wins the war.

How does the motor of insight work and rev? For without pragmatism and applicability, insight as concept remains an inefficient and idling abstraction. My psychotic experiences oftentimes, but not always, revolve around common themes. The themes very often involve thoughts, beliefs, and feelings of persecution. And although I understand this theme quite well, please do not misconstrue. The experience nonetheless remains disturbing when in the midst. Insight does not indicate the absence of disturbing experiences, but it does indicate the management of the disturbance. And with management comes life-affirmed.

Insight dwells in the cognitive and derives from experience. Its denomination is retrospection. I habitually review and classify my psychotic experiences by characteristic and trait. I identify my distortions and challenge my presumptive beliefs. I think about all that occurred, and I critically reason. I sieve and parse. I integrate and analyze. I construct and deconstruct. Then, when satisfied with my conclusions, I discard the remains and get on with life. This was not always the case. I used to hold on to my psychotic experiences as calamities. But no longer. I have learned to let go of my adversities. I retain the lesson but not the wound. Such experiences now drift into the past with greater ease. And this allows for persistence and sustenance.

When experiencing a current episode of psychosis, the delusional theme may be common and understood but to the psychotic mind it nevertheless presents as true at the time of its presentation. This typical cognitive binary dualism is again exemplary of the inherent paradox to schizophrenia. The psychotic perception may look like a duck and quack like a duck but in fact is no such foul. The perception appears indubitably true and therefore comes with the correlated feelings of persecution and psychological disturbance. It is at this point that I used to dwell, but it is no longer. Now I retrospect and develop ideas that will enhance my coping for the future. I used to fixate and ruminate. Now I learn and let go. I have become comfortable with perceptual ambiguity. I have become comfortable on the fence of reality.

Insight can occur on both the macro and micro levels. On the macro level, the concern is for the whole, while on the micro level it is for the parts. For our purposes, the whole is schizophrenia and the parts are the symptoms. I have offered some ideas on the whole and now more on the parts. There are many symptoms that qualify as parts to the constituted whole of schizophrenia, but I promise you, my dear reader, I will not mechanically address each symptom one by one in an automated mechanical churning of script. Too boring, I heed! I say, let's keep things most loosely tied and fear not the occasional literary meandering!

Psychosis is simply a cohort of symptoms. You may wonder, if I am familiar with the symptoms and have good insight, why then does psychosis persist and recur? This is a good and logical question and it comes with a rebuttal. At times, my mind is restful, quiet, and void of psychosis. I am not psychotic at all times. Sometimes, however, my mind is not quiet. It becomes incrementally frenetic. During psychosis, my mind must fastidiously attend to its symptoms that arrive with force and persuasion. It is routine for me to hallucinate persecutory voices. These auditory hallucinations will commingle with persecutory delusions in mutual reinforcement. The delusions and hallucinations come accompanied by feelings of severe paranoia and persecution. With such a mixture, I further wrestle with hopelessness and dysphoria. Schizophrenia will then nonchalantly introduce a few more novel symptoms with associated existential quagmires resulting in an absolute pummeling inundation. The creative outcome equates to a most challenging existential gestalt, and answer to question, makes psychological riddance a most difficult task. That is, at least for the time being. Give me some time, however, and I will answer the bell.

I fluctuate between the poles of rational quietude and psychotic freneticism; day one, temperance, day two, psychosis. Firstly settled, secondly disturbed. I often wonder how from quietude can come inundation. When absent of psychosis, I have learned to remain alert and guarded for potential triggers. Sometimes my defensive measures can quash a potential psychotic episode. Nevertheless, despite such guardedness, symptoms routinely find measure to penetrate my psychological fortress. From quietude, suddenly a symptom will flash. Perhaps, let's say, an auditory hallucination. At this point, my serene tabula rasa becomes menaced, but, by and large, things remain yet manageable. Upon first presentation I will self-talk "I just heard a voice, I just hallucinated." Generally, in the midst of my otherwise quiet and rational mind, a singular symptom does not drown. So at this point, my buoyancy remains, and I wade on in the day's activity. At the same time, however, I have also learned not to be so entirely cognitively indifferent or attitudinally lackadaisical. From a macro perspective, I now know all too well that the singular symptom can quickly turn plural by the simple course of a temporal whimsy.

At this precarious point, things can go in two divergent directions. The first can skew to rationality and the auditory hallucination can be but an isolated shout from the dark. This is the favorable outcome. The second possibility involves an insidious proliferation. With this direction comes the subtle progression of ever-increasing symptoms over time. Slowly and incrementally, my mind begins to skew towards irrationality and psychosis. The perilous gains momentum. The single auditory hallucination lays fertile ground for the next. One hallucination then becomes followed by the next. The time between each diminishes and a regularity ensues. Delusions emerge accompanied by feelings of persecution and paranoia. The symptoms effectively replicate and psychosis moves to the forefront of my mind. The descent into madness starts benignly enough but soon metastasizes in a contagious frenzy of associated symptoms. And by means of a devilish persuasion, psychosis lays claim to a temporal grounding. My reality shifts from quietude to symptomatic and a spectral psychosis reveals again.

Insight does not indicate the absence of psychosis. Psychosis emerges unconditionally. When psychotic, my mind becomes like two battering rams. Disturbing experiences ensue. I fight for rationality in lieu of hellish psychotic states. Two divergent realities seem equally possible. The one is existentially benign, and the other is psychotic hell. The two realities oppose but both seem viable. I simply cannot differentiate. Therefore, in response to this recurring ambiguity, I have acquired some skills. Firstly, I have learned a dispositional comfort amid discomfort. And secondly, follows a bit of cognitive trickery. I pause my mind's eye midway to the the point of the opposing realities. And here it is, I psychologically tread. Whilst my cognitive treading, I then remind to breathe, and deeply so. And with deep breath, I then patiently wait for the acuity to pass. Sometimes my consequential experiences become fairly comfortable. At other times, not so much. I find, however, no need to rigorously self-hash regarding symptomatic detail or minutia since thus far, by this manner, I have found a sufficient sustenance. And so I persist, and gosh, irrevocably, would you believe the sun rises yet again!

Sometimes I just know I am going to remain psychotic for months at a time. This is based on experience. Knowing this is helpful, as I give myself proverbial permission to be psychotic for the time being. I tell myself I am having a temporal psychosis, but I also dovetail the additional notion that in time my rationality will return. This relieves the pressure, so I can remain a most cool cucumber (my dear reader, remember not to take this or life too seriously since levity is essential to sustenance). I allow myself the crucial variable of time. For some inexplicable reason, I can often rightly intuit that I will be psychotic for a few months. I just know it at an instinctual level. I suppose this is an example of insight. I also know instinctively at this point in my illness that I will eventually return to rationality. And this is the value of variable time. In my instance, the euphemism of "time heals all wounds" transcends the cliché and holds a most considerable and wise salve.

At times, the emergence of psychosis is slow and subtle. Other times, however, its declaration is abrupt, particularly following a significant "trigger." Trigger is the clinical term used to refer to the phenomenon that sets off, or triggers, symptoms of a mental illness. Specified symptoms, combined with the associative experiences, potentiate as triggers. Certain auditory hallucinations and formative delusions both exemplify. When I am sufficiently triggered, settled and quiet quickly turns frenetic and psychotic. I inevitably get that sinking feeling in my stomach followed by an immediate and most remarkable shift of perception. My disposition quickly transmutes from **euthymic** and rational to paranoid and psychotic. A sequelae of disturbing perceptions and dystonic emotions ensue, and my experience feels out of control. After such an immediate trigger, it usually takes a bit of time to adjust to my new psychosis.

Psychosis presents to my mind primarily in the following two manners: slow and insidious or immediate and abrupt. Both are disconcerting, and I find no favor in either manner of arrival. My stern objective always is to cast aside my cognitive pathologies as quickly and definitively as my intellect will allow. And thus far, without exception, a return to rationality from psychosis has been repeatedly achievable given time, insight, and a good dose of abiding faith.

Customarily, by a temporal measure, my return to a stable rationality from an episodic psychosis comes with an unpredictable variance. A recent personal experience will exemplify. While at work, I could be found quiet and sane. But then enter, actor, menacing hallucination. From status stable, my mind leapt into an immediate psychosis accompanied by its usual cohorts of paranoia and psychological vertigo. In this instance. following this particular trigger, psychosis and I buddied for several weeks before the symptoms began to abate. As symptoms dissipate over time, due in part to my processing of events and use of insight, my mind begins to quiet again with returns to temperance and rationality, Insight, therefore, is analogous to the sum total of an equation. It involves knowing the parts (symptoms) as well as the whole (diagnosis). Insight includes an understanding of the variables of the illness. Variables can include such factors as the symptoms, symptom duration, onset variables, failed and successful coping means, medication choices, protective factors, the influence of stress, the use of treatment resources, hopefulness versus despair, knowledge of symptom remediation, benefits and costs of socialization, and the generalized ability to recover and do so as quickly as possible. I have learned that sometimes patience is required. And at this point in my illness, unlike earlier on, I can now live in psychotic states for extended periods of time with the continuance of efficacious functioning including at work and in leisure.

When actively symptomatic, I have learned the fine art of psychotic obfuscation. During psychosis, I have learned to strictly self-monitor my words and actions. Despite my disturbance, I am diligent in maintaining a decorum of rationality. I am vigilant of my behaviors and language. I do not stray outside of the rational context. This allows me to ably function while psychotic. I suspect the quality of my functioning suffers in the least, but its diminishment is negligible. Amid psychosis, debilitation is now forlorn and all life activity remains integral. I have psychologically normalized my psychosis and I have attained a hard-fought truce. Psychosis continues. but I have learned a good deal to ignore its perceptions, despite its vexing bark. I have learned the paramount skill of maintaining a behavioral rationality during a cognitive irrationality. Schizophrenia proffered its requisition and glinted its false fangs, and I have responded in kind by Tao and insight. I hold insight as necessary and essential. It is my recourse.

My last thoughts on insight must include mention of a most crucial psychological concept that demands a thorough comprehension. There is a clinical term called "**anosognosia**." Anosognosia is used to describe the phenomenon of a prevailing lack of insight. Some individuals suffer madness with no self-awareness into their own irrationalities or of their distinct disconnect from the greater reality. This is a significant subset of the thought disorder population. In these instances, with no insight into one's psychosis, complete recovery is impossible. If one were to have a conversation with an actively psychotic individual who is entirely absent of any insight, the madness would be observably overt and unquestionable to those of rational mind. In such individuals, bizarre topics will emerge, and behavior and speech will be highly erratic and irrational. Many who carry anosognosia dwell in a persistent psychosis with no availing return to the rational faculties. In these cases, treatment adopts a different foci with indications beyond matters of a developmental insight.

The best outcomes for those with anosognosia are characteristically deleterious. Much of the care revolves around harm-reduction, safety considerations, and eliminating any undue emotional distress. Often, such individuals are capable of sitting for hours absent from any requisite stimulation, i.e., social activity, conversations, TV, etc. Some may exhibit catatonic-like behavior from day to month to year. Those with anosognosia can also be more prone to violence and of repeated violations of social norms. The consequences of these type of behaviors often involves repeated psychiatric hospitalizations and/or incarcerations. Some with this presentation can become institutionalized in the mental health or criminal justice systems for long periods. Those who escape these unfortunate outcomes often do so at the behest of heroic family efforts. Anosognosia is clinically understood as an altogether different psychiatric presentation with significantly different outcome skews. Therefore, anosognosia is a most necessary a priori differentiation and discernment when considering one's ability or capacity to construct an insight with a characteristic salve and remediable acumen.

And with that said, I say adieu, adios, and goodbye in a most mercifully manner to my meandering diatribe concerning the complex concept of insight. I hope I sufficiently detailed the value of insight, for it is the essential pragmatic genesis to effectively cope with schizophrenia and the primary psychological conduit to ultimately conquering schizophrenia. But our journey does not end here for we have yet to reach our fated and illumined destiny. So shed any lingering doubts, my dear reader, for our light is now available to the eye and together we now step with a hopeful and spirited anticipation.

13

Psychological Assimilation

Vis-a-vis of having personal experiences marked by both rationality and irrationality, I would like to return to the macro concept of "reality." Having experiences that are both rational and psychotic in nature presents as bit of a metaphysical quandary. If I can have such a variance in my experiences across the spectrum of rationality/irrationality, what then is in fact the nature of this thing we call reality? As I earlier detailed, reality is a collective enterprise, and as such it exudes in the space between people. Reality is not a fixed entity. Rather, it is an authentic social construction implicitly governed by a consensus tacit agreement. Reality is a supremely radical concept but nevertheless is accepted and agreed-upon by its constituents with a most curious ease and allowance. For some, I suppose metaphysical reality is never questioned with much earnestness. "It is what it is" and any further consideration beyond this euphemistic truism belies of nothing more than an inert intellectual dalliance. I suppose for many there is a kind of natural acquiescence to the terms of reality. And why not? For what is to doubt when the terms of reality universally abide spanning the life course? In my instance, however, because of recurrent psychosis, reality per se translates to a linguistic misnomer. Any such abidance to a certified reality is found lacking. Consequently, I have a persistent nag concerning what is real and what is not, or what is truth and what is not. Because of psychosis, reality has taken on a different texture. But why would I think otherwise? It necessarily follows from my experience.

    I, too, cognitively process and function in the shared conglomerate of reality. Our very ability to relate to one another and function amongst each other is fundamentally and dutifully bound by the implicit constructs of our shared reality. Absent of these implicit constructs, reality would be chaotic and dysfunctional. Relationships would be subject to instability and unpredictability. Efficient societal functioning would disintegrate. Civilization would dissolve. Ultimately, reality would require a radical reinterpretation.

I am not resistant to our collective reality. In fact, it is much the pleasure. But additionally, my experiences with psychosis leads me to conclude that the truth for my personal reality is not solely contained in the rational shared reality. I have had so many experiences outside of the rational shared reality that I have developed some additional thoughts, even beliefs, about the fabric of my personal reality.

What are the characteristics of my reality that rest outside of the rational shared reality? For utilitarian purposes, I will label this as my "personal reality," which in total deviates at times from shared reality. The description of my personal reality is best begun with the introduction of the term of "concept." Understanding how I intend this term is primary. Concepts are base. They are the content before my observing mind. All that exists, exists as concept. All things under the sun, and including the sun, exist as concept. Physical objects, interpersonal relationships, thoughts, emotions, beliefs, nature, animals, and language all present as concepts to my mind.

My mind and consciousness function by recognizing, evaluating, and contemplating presenting concepts. Certainly there are an infinitude of potential concepts, including in an infinitude of combinations. Concepts present to my mind as variables and they change over time. In trying to make sense of my issues with psychosis, I have concluded that concepts play a most fundamental role as the primary constituents to my characteristic personal reality.

Psychosis is inherently a metaphysical illness. Its malaise is rendered through the concept of reality. As such, psychosis has triggered in me a most persistent preoccupation with macro-metaphysics. I find this preoccupation, however, to be a most unexpected blessing. In a most circumstantial manner, impositional psychosis has ultimately led to derivative metaphysical conviction. And I have found attributable conviction to be most reputable type of life ideal.

At one time the characteristic normative shared reality was soundly foundational to my experience. My experiences were normative and inclusive to agreed-upon shared reality. I had no reason to doubt this shared reality. But with the onset of psychosis, normative shared reality was no longer all-inclusive to my experiences. As a result, metaphysical preoccupation germinated.

Prior to psychosis, when fully participatory and uniquely accepting of our collective reality, I had no inkling that reality could contain anything much beyond my normative experiences. Prior to the first onset of psychosis, although I studied philosophy, I really was not in any manner a practitioner of philosophy. I enjoyed philosophical ideas and conclusions as good intellectual and academic fodder, but in practical terms philosophy did not play a utilitarian role in my life. I certainly did not subject myself and my experiences to any type of regular philosophic methodology or inquiry. I had no Descartes or Sartre in my soul. Due to this lack of philosophic rigor, my normative experiences were the obvious reality and it presented as indubious. Why would I doubt normative reality without any just cause? In other words, in my mind, prior to psychotic experiences, reality was indubitably the shared, socially constructed, and tacitly agreed-upon reality. Any other hypothesized realities were simply abstract philosophies by philosophic intellectuals. Reality was normative, and I had no doubts. I had no consistent outlier experiences beyond the collective reality. But then entered experiences marked by psychosis. With such experiences alternatives emerged to the normative shared reality. And why not, for my experiences were in fact not shared with others. Apparently, reality, or shall I say my personal reality, was something different than the seemingly impermeable persistent shared reality. So after an inundation of psychotic experiences with routine frequencies external to the normative shared reality, I have had to reevaluate what is real to me. And in fact, the new framework for my personal reality is surprisingly philosophical, including in a utilitarian manner.

I have termed my personal metaphysics as "conceptual reality." My conceptual reality is inclusive to shared normative reality and also takes into consideration experiences labeled as psychotic. How do I define conceptual reality? Conceptual reality is the viewpoint that the "metaphysical all" presents to my mind by manner and form of a sequelae of variable concepts. It is the interplay of my mind and that which presents to my mind. Mind is the constant and that which presents to my mind are the variables. I prefer to label the variables as the "concepts of mind." Concepts take multitudes of forms and presentations to my mind in the like of thoughts, affects, visualizations, physical representations, ideas, beliefs, other individuals, myself as subject and object, words, language, and imagination. Surely this is not all that can present to my mind, but it is a good beginning. It is not my intent, however, to describe conceptual reality in a detailed or comprehensive manner since it is but an associated ancillary to the pertinent primary. I mention my theory mostly to illustrate how I have psychologically integrated the foreign body of psychosis into my prevailing psychological whole. Therefore, in regards to my theoretical conceptual reality, the textual indication defaults to status brevity.

Conceptual reality is my specified metaphysical theory. Generalized metaphysical theory may be better understood by the euphemistic phrasing known as "the **theory of everything**." The unified theory of everything is the metaphysical holy grail. It has not yet been achieved and it remains the ever-elusive target to all serious metaphysical theorists. The most current ideas pertaining to the theory of everything involve such fields as string theory and quantum physics, along with their derivatives. These theories are characteristically mathematical and the elite practitioners on the cutting edge of these theories casually approach or leisurely exceed the requisites of intellectual genius.

In my theoretical metaphysical universe, concepts are the variables of reality and the concepts are grounded by the constant, that being my mind. My conception of reality therefore is inclusive to shared reality and also explains my psychotic states. My mind remains constant but the concepts which present to my mind remain variable. The concepts of my mind are at times synchronized with mutually shared reality, but additionally, are also at times not in sync with said reality and are characteristic of psychotic thought. In this manner, my personal conceptual reality accounts for both the rational and psychotic, and therefore the whole to my experience remains integral.

My personal conceptual reality takes the form in part of a solipsistic framework but also with key differentiations. Solipsism is the reductionist theory that offers that reality solely exists within the parameters of one's mind. Or euphemistically put, it's "all in your head." Solipsism is considered reductionist because it postulates no binding correspondence to anything outside of mind (or outside of one's own head). This includes other sentient beings, the environment, and/or "physical" objects (like chairs, or the TV, or a stone). For example, the chair only exists in my mind. It does not exist in the "external" environment. It is solely a product of my mind. There is no internal/external differentiation because it is simply a matter of mind proper. My conceptual reality differs from solipsism, however, in at least a few manners.

My conceptual reality, along with its solipsistic traits, also includes a **nihilistic** component. Admittedly, I have this nagging intuition that there may be no actual correspondence from that of one's mind to its perceived external contents. Perhaps reality is indeed nothing more than the fodder that presents before one's mind. But I think there are a few considerations lacking with solipsism. Firstly, solipsism takes the existence of mind as a given or as a first truth. Of this I am not too sure. Secondly, solipsism does not fully account for a macro creator, or God, if you will. My conceptual reality, alternatively, considers both factors.

It is dubious to me that my mind necessarily exists. Additionally, I must also consider what I believe to be the primary question and consideration above all else- that being the idea of a creator or God. But before proceeding further, my leaning disposition toward this specified metaphysical theme grows fond of an intellectual stall. I really do not want to bore regarding the details and vagaries of my personal philosophy in a comprehensive and most logical manner. So, at this time, I will get to the point in favor of a further mechanistic churning (as you know, my dear reader, I would rather churn butter than engage in rote scribing). For the sake of brevity, therefore, I offer the following conclusions. My "conceptual reality" exists as the constant of mind and it's presenting variable concepts. There is no necessary external correspondence to the representations of mind. Additionally, I can also doubt the existence of my own mind (much the difference to Descartes). Further, the possibility or even the likelihood of a creator remains a formidable consideration. Therefore, my conceptual reality reduces to the following traits: my mind, that in itself is dubious, along with its ever-variable contents that take the form of concepts. The contents of mind, or its conceptions, are also dubious as necessarily existent. Descartes could not doubt his own mind and his own thoughts. I, however, can doubt both. And this is thus without exception due to my recurring issues with psychosis. Therefore, all without exception is dubious. But let me not be judged as entirely philosophically skeptical for my theory as yet comes with an extractable tangibility including unabashed assertions and steadfast convictions. So stay tuned, my dear reader.

I believe conceptual reality to be held together by a force that binds all in support of a greater inferred psychic–environmental totality. This psychic-environmental reality is dubious but nevertheless appears correlated and unified. Unfortunately, this apparent connectivity is also dubious. Therefore, reality reduces to an absolute dubiousness, including mind, its variables, and any necessary psychic-environmental correspondence. And with that, I arrive at the bus stop of **philosophical skepticism**, i.e., all is in doubt, including doubt itself. This relegates my theory to the interminable constraints of a cantankerous logical fallacy by manner of its impotent circularity. But at this point of coherent peril, my theory does not yet yield. For to reach my anticipated theoretical destination, one last step, or shall I say leap, is required. In my search for metaphysical reality and prevailing truth, my path has been of duration and obstacle. But my path is not without destiny. So where do I turn amid all this doubt and logical circularity? From my singular vantage point the answer abounds with clarity, transcends all doubt, and seeps with certitude. And it is with a most exhausted exhilaration that I finally arrive at my destination. It is a destiny reached via a most grueling course, but who am I to offer any quibble of arrival when my shining urn unveils before my very eyes? My metaphysical journey, supported by an unrelenting schizophrenia, finds its ultimatum and it resides on a steep. I attest, it is here I find God. I have long sought light to shed the psychological dark. And with confluence and destination, it is He whom is the illumined, and He casts no shadows.

14

Divine Intervention

The foremost consideration pertaining to the God concept is unquestionably that of existence. And so metaphysics begins anew at its inherent primary occupation regarding the problem of existence. Pertaining to God, we now enter the realm of **theological metaphysics** with its focus on the proof or disproof of a divine existence. The query therefore of "does God exist" becomes the instigate to the ardent theologian and the genesis to derivative theological theory or offerings. From this most fundamental query sources the fountainhead to any further theological metaphysics.

Pertaining to God's existence, I will offer my conclusion then followed by its reasoning. For millennials, no definitive theological resolution of absolute certainty has been achieved pertaining to a divine existence. In other words, God's existence remains thoroughly speculative and thus far without definitive answer, at least that is from a scientific perspective. But I ask, why should God's existence be any more or less certain than my own? I certainly can doubt my own existence as perhaps merely some sort of dream-state or lasting apparition. Therefore, are not similar doubts to be expected pertaining to God's existence?

When considering the God concept, disparity and dissent reign by perspective. Ocular diversity abounds. And from the eye of this diversity comes weighted consequence to the collective human gestalt. The concept of God creates a fracture in the mutually and tacitly agreed-upon socially constructed reality. The concept of God is generally not collectively agreed upon in any universal capacity. In fact, I would dare say, the mutually and tacitly agreed upon socially constructed reality is more unified in consensus than to any posit regarding

God's existence or nonexistence. The human code prevails in its characteristic collectivity. Nevertheless, my intent is not of a generalized hypothesis in favor of a theological ontology. Rather, I would like to simply broach the God concept by manner and purview of personal experience.

Theological ontology has persisted for ages, and its canon will persist for many more. But oftentimes when there is a significant quandary or issue yet to be solved, it is due to the cause of "asking the wrong question." If an answer remains elusive, the question may be wrong. Scientific factualism is rigorous by this process. Albert Einstein was the very best at asking the "right," or be it, the better questions and, as such, he was transformative. Ensuring prudent questions is a weighted parcel to the process of scientific methodology and ultimately to the emergence of scientific "fact."

Many issues go unsolved for significant periods of time, centuries even, due to defunct questions opportune for intellectual cul-de-sac. Einstein, however, was the embodiment of better questions. When considering the fabric of reality, including such concepts as light, gravity, time, and energy, Einstein left behind prior hypotheses and asked different questions. He was famous for his inventive and ingenious thought experiments. By asking different questions, along with his innate genius, he was revolutionary. Einstein asked better questions, and when considering the concept of God, I follow the great Einstein by methodology.

Simply put, there is no universal consensus regarding God. There are too many variables in the concept for universal agreement, at least at this given time. Questions and variables abound regarding the God concept. Does God exist? Is there one God or many? Is your God the same as my God? What is God's nature? How did God come into existence? Is there an afterlife dependent on God's existence? And certainly, this is just the tip of the iceberg. Further yet include the humanistic and atheist perspectives regarding man's existence and any consensus about God or not God are even further muddled.

Wise questions are critical when developing a hypothesis in furtherance of improved understanding and potential solutions. In this vein, my question concerning God is not of existence. I also have no interest in necessarily joining an already established consensus based on their derivative conclusions. I am simply focused on how the God concept pertains to my existence and my experience. I think the inherent questions concerning God are best asked by each. I find the concept best approached specifically, not generally. And if our derivatives merge, bully. And if they diverge, bully again. After all, the God concept is so uniquely personal that differences must be expected, and perhaps appreciated. Therefore, upon these considerations, this leads to my specific question. What is the role of God in my life?

With the onus of God's proven existence removed by means of a differentiated question, and in lieu of a necessitated coherent theological ontology, I am now free to explore the God concept absent of the constraints of a mandated generalizable conclusion. With this liberation, allow me to define the concept of God as it relates to my experience. This definition and description may be similar to yours, or it may not be. I don't intend to reach consensus. God, like many crucial life considerations, I find to be a highly personal issue. It is an issue of choice, an issue of belief or not, and certainly an issue worthy of contemplation. Consensus is not the target here but rather I seek and offer answers as solely derivative of a singular human experiential existence. The definition then of God in my life experience is such. God is my creator. I have long thought about the issue of how I came into being. In my mind, it is possible that in some manner that I created myself and inserted myself into this being-in-the-world based on a deliberate choice borne of some sort of necessity. Perhaps I am my own creator. Perhaps it was necessary on my part to insert myself into this being-in-the-world without the a posteriori knowledge that I am in fact my own creator. Perhaps I did so to experience "life" per se, or perhaps for some other salient reasons. I find this line of thinking possible, but not believable. As such, I leave it disavowed.

With this denial, then follows the idea of a personal creator. I am seemingly placed here in space-time, with self-awareness, and with perceptions of being among others. These others, "humans" by verbiage, are seemingly in similar-type circumstances also situated in space-time and are amongst my company as well. And it is from this specified metaphysical context that I intuitively leap. Like an unstable electron jumping shells, I arrive at the easeful conviction of the necessity of a creator (or creators). I simply cannot shun this dimensional presence, including being in the company of like others. I must de facto conclude that creation is necessitated. Existence proper necessitates creation. Items cannot exist void of creation. Therefore, genesis and creation are but one.

With such an arrival, follows my conviction. I was created by another, and that other is the term I use for God. I choose to believe in one creator versus the plural. To me, this eliminates interminable confusion including a pesky infinite regress both of which skew an otherwise coherent rationality. As a differentiated entity, God's manufactured appearance comes with inherent ambiguity. I find His essence beyond the parameters of both resolute distinction and human reason. But conjunct to this ambiguity, also comes the fountainhead of a personified divinity. Such an incarnate comes by the presence and appearance of "Jesus

Christ." By form Jesus, the somewhat nebulous divine transmutes to a qualitative revelation. And although distinct, the holy essence in toto nevertheless persists with some obscurity.

After Christ's crucifixion, he ascended from his grave and returned to his celestial positioning, and in manner the personification of deity was again transformed. Upon ascension, the human form was left behind, and divinity returned to the spiritual and ethereal realms. Jesus thusly becomes allegorically placed at the right hand of his father once again transcendent of space-time. Nevertheless, Jesus in name temporally persists as an exemplary offering of divine incarnate.

I perceive God in a dualistic manner. I apprehend God both as personified and transcendent of personification. God may also take presence beyond my scope and apprehension. When personified, I think of God as male by gender. This notion is similarly conceived of in Catholic Bible, that being, of the like of a male father figure, i.e., God the Father Almighty. Admittedly, I find this notion of a gendered God intriguing. This belief of God, as masculinely personified, is currently pervasive including across cultures. Why does God necessarily present as personified in the masculine gender? I find it most interesting insofar as potential implications. Being male, when praying or when in dialogue with God, the relationship is gender consistent. But when a female relates to God, it is not gender consistent. I wonder if this carries any pertinent dynamic. Further, given God's essence as transcendent, why not gender transcendent? But of this I do not mash, for these are but the queries of detail. I remain rightly copasetic, for an enduring faith is but a predicate to the wholly unknown.

I find God to be omnipotent and omniscient. I know this to be most cliché but at the same time I do not find it passé. I experience God as all-loving and all-good. I believe God participates in my life with influence, guidance, and support. God implores me to virtuosity, kindness, and goodness. When I do not meet these expectations, I repent and seek his wisdom. My relationship with God is intimately personal and singularly unique. In my relationship with God, he has a tremendous sense of humor as far as his participation and intentions in my life. God often presents himself for my witness in the most humorous of manners and appearances. And lastly, God presents himself to my mind in many a mysterious way, but also in such discernible manners and means that I find doubting his existence a most forlorn possibility.

The quality of God I find most endearing is his comic manner in my life. While amidst a handful of my specified psychotic episodes, when I have found myself experientially interacting with God, the tone and tenor of the exchange inevitably becomes most amusing and just plain darn funny! God's mannerist joie de vivre is exuberantly comical to my most attentive mind. Not in a millennials time could I ever personally conjure such a characteristic relationship. His manner of approach is as an everyday commoner and, as such, his existential juxtaposition becomes intolerably comical. God's council is unanimously simply stated with a timbre of intended humor. His words are sage, and his delivery explodes with humor and love. Perhaps He has deemed by this accord that I am best reached.

As a child, I was raised in the Catholic faith. I routinely attended church and religious education. I met all the timely milestones for the Catholic sacraments. I am most grateful and appreciative for my faith-based upbringing. As I grew into adulthood, however, my religious activity weaned; that is, until the timely application of reading the Catholic Bible. I had always considered the Bible a most prominent document worthy of a thorough investigation. I also knew the Bible to be a most meticulous read and a significantly time-intensive endeavor. But since I was unemployed, I decided the timing was right and I took to task (as a sidebar to the unemployed, having no job can be blissful given the right disposition and hyperbolic perspective). Cover to cover, The Old Testament through The New Testament, it took me several months of daily attention and determination to definitively conclude a most challenging document. I now consider the Bible the preeminent read of my life. It is a transcendent text beyond mere spiritualism. Its continued bearance on human affairs and human contextualism cannot be underestimated. Its relevance and influence holds sway to our modernity. Its explanatory power is superlative.

I consider the Bible amongst the greatest of all written texts. And with this literary categorization, I began to reflect of my opines vis-a-vis the greatest of all authors, of any era or time. And in a most non-mechanized and nonlinear manner, I excitedly offer you, my dear reader, some of those I consider the very best of all literary authorship. My one caveat to the listing is that I do not generally read literary fiction, so my offering is limited to nonfiction. I offer the following list as some of the greatest thinkers and writers across all cultures and all ages. I consider the greatest to include: Socrates, Plato, Aristotle, Kierkegaard, Kant, Hume, Descartes, Sartre, Nietzsche, Dostoevsky, Voltaire, Ken Wilber, Gregory Bateson, Sigmund Freud, Carl Jung, Thomas Aquinas, Suzuki, Osho, Heidegger, C.S. Lewis, Dante, Bertrand Russell, Bohm, Einstein, and Marx. Certainly, this is not a comprehensively exhaustive list but rather simply an off-the-cuff brainstorm solely for purposes of fun. I recommend all these authors for your most leisurely perusal, my dear reader, and each according to your own specified personal interests.

Returning to topic, over the last few years, I have attended mass on a few occasions. Prior to reading the Bible, the ceremonial mass was a psychological nag. During its course, I would repeatedly question ceremonial intent and relevance. But with its read, the ceremonial mass of the Catholic faith is now well understood both by form and process. In other words, the mass makes sense now, and this comes with great consolation.

It is well-known clinically that oftentimes psychosis can include theological themes alongside spiritual or religious experiences. Certainly, this does not pertain to all with psychosis but for some it is common. Most often, psychiatrists and clinicians will categorize such experiences as "delusional" and as secondary to psychosis. I certainly understand the reasoning to such a finding and it is a most legitimate and rational conclusion. When I am engaged in my professional capacity, I too will denote in my clinical notes "delusions marked by religiosity" when a patient speaks of non normative spiritual perceptions or experiences. A clinically firm differentiated boundary pertaining to that which is delusionally based as opposed to reality-based is a most necessary therapeutic consideration. Overly flexible clinical latitudes inevitably lead to logical fallacy, and as such becomes counterproductive to the well-being of the patient. In other words, if a therapist consents to delusionally based patient-reported content as part of the reality construct, then all becomes possible with no delineations between reality and not reality. Such a therapist becomes an unwitting participant in the "all or nothing" logical fallacy and as such does a disservice to the seeking patient.

Through a most gruesome trial and error process, I have learned a most necessary cognitive skill in conquering schizophrenia. De facto, I have developed the ability to view my psychotic experiences from both the objective clinical perspective and also from my subjective experiential perspective. This binary knowledge is contributory to my generalized insight. One does not need to be a therapist to understand the clinical component to schizophrenia, but when conquering schizophrenia, one sure as heck should be able to think like one! For one to heal and to move beyond the turmoil of psychosis, understanding the muddled but differentiated boundary between reality and psychosis is a most sturdy requisite. Without this arcane knowledge capable functioning in all life realms will be most elusive. I cannot emphasize enough how important it is to be self-aware of the presence of a personal psychosis while simultaneously maintaining a self-aware behavioral rationality. And to be able to consistently accomplish this behavioral trick is the absolute game changer!

Psychotic experiences must be understood from two perspectives. And most intriguingly and beguilingly, these perspectives are oppositional. When psychotic, I must cognitively parse with a capable self-talk. I must remind and prod, "I see, but I do not...I hear, but I do not...it is, but it is not." Lest I forget, my perceptual faculties are bruised and broken. If I believe what I perceive, then follows the fool. Psychosis, therefore, can only be mitigated by the maintenance of a dualistic awareness. In the end, "it is real, but it is not." This again is the embedded paradox inherent of schizophrenia.

15

Uhh...Hello God?!

An adage regales man is most alive by course of his passions. Schizophrenia perpetually stirs my emotions. Its nature is passionate, if not misguided. It blends a taste for metaphysical appeal, and comes with a certain incline to the divine. Are the religious experiences of an individual with schizophrenia simply delusional, or of another quality, or perhaps of some varied combination?

Similarly to clinical professionals and perhaps those of the general population, I too can discount my personal religious experiences as wholly delusional by manner and use of my insight. Nevertheless, my religious experiences present with such a great vibrancy that I also choose to retain an additional perspective. In my perusals of quantum physics, if there is one item I have gleaned, it is the understanding that the classical "and/or" metaphysical paradigm is now largely antiquated in favor of the quantum "both/and" metaphysical paradigm. I can certainly understand the delusional taint of my spiritual experiences but at the same time the theological meaning acoustically abounds, and I choose not to lend deaf ear. I attest, experiences marked by a communion with Divinity are not easily discarded. Vis-à-vis, therefore, I simply choose the "both/and," rather the "either/or."

My most recent religious experience occurred just a few months ago. While I was working, I was amid delusion, hallucination, and paranoia amongst other typical symptoms and my day was off to its customary angsty prologue. This episodic psychosis was quite overwhelming, and I was mightily engaged in attempting to keep any level of sanity and rationality. When floridly psychotic, as during this episode, I feel a sense of tremendous stress, especially when experiencing persecutory delusions. The continuance of competent functioning with underlying persecutory feelings is perhaps the most challenging trial of my schizophrenia. Perceptions of social isolation and collusive persecution by others can be terrorizing. The inherent stress to the perceived predicament further exacerbates my already distorted perceptions. My symptoms accumulate and the moments intensify. The experience approaches unmanageability. Any possible means of safe escape becomes my primary cognitive occupation. My perceived breaking point approaches the periphery. Thick feelings of hopelessness emerge. I try not to succumb and I gather myself one last time.

Intriguingly, on a most rare occasion, from such a typical symptomatic apex can ensue a psychological brilliance. Either sourced **ex nihilo** or from the depths of despair, of which the two I am not so sure, suddenly exalts Divine proclamation. His means are variable, but God reveals. And with His presence follows religious experience.

My most recent religious experience occurred about three months prior to this writing. I was at work well-attired in persecutory delusions and immersed in a deep hopelessness. I believed my fate and destiny were sealed. Suddenly, however, from my utter darkness the miraculous occurred. A coworker entered my office to socialize for a bit as by routine we often chatted. She sat down and started conversing with me about a work issue followed by a known personal issue. But moments into our conversation, I experienced the perceptual recognizance of the divine incarnate. The young woman with whom I was speaking suddenly was shroud in a divine presence. My perceptions indicated I was with God personified. My faculties indicated the spiritually Divine. Is it possible that God would present in my life in such an existential manner? During this brief religious experience, my impression was God personified Himself, and He did so to provoke me from my despair. The content of the conversation was ordinary. The manner of the conversation was remarkable.

The woman's disposition was innocent; her demeanor, good and pure. I remember thinking, "you are God?" I perceived her to be God personified. I don't know how my mind arrives at such a conclusion of Divine incarnate, but these experiences and perceptions are strikingly vivid. Additionally, these perceptions are so securely bound to an abiding sense of faith that a Divine veracity exudes and as such I experience God. These experiences lack dubiousness and become assertively time-stamped on my intellect with a characteristic psychological certainty.

I again thought "you are God," but this time it was a statement and not a question. Like a lightening bolt, it pierced my intellect, "I am conversing with

God." This ideation lasted about five minutes, and as usual, it was thoroughly convincing. Then, like always, it abruptly ended. The coworker left, and there I sat once again wondering what the heck just happened. The interaction definitively restored my ailing heart but how could it be? Did God just personify Himself and do quick corrective work on my despairing soul? Ostensibly, God appeared, fixed my malaise, and left (perhaps to continue his work elsewhere). Is it possible? Is it possible what I experienced was God? By a conservative measure, I estimate about ten such distinct religious experiences. And I am always left pondering the possibility. I do not seek these experiences and I do not will these experiences. They occur unexpectedly and absent of deliberation. But no doubt, they do happen. And so I wonder yet again.

I do not run to the hills with proclamations following a religious experience. I have learned, from experiential trial and error, that in response to such experiences to practice a quick temperamental sobriety accompanied by an acute psychological temperance. I have also learned to keep my yap-trap securely fastened for any such topical discussions only come with peril and not fruit. I do this for my generalized well-being and psychological stability. I heed most cautiously. I keep these experiences internal. I do not share or relate these experiences to others since it is really no matter to anyone beyond myself. I do not seek reinforcement from others nor do I seek refutation. I simply come to my own conclusions and this suffices.

Without fail and absent of any, all my experiences involving a temporal-spatial transactional exchange with God eventually come with a comical overtone. In other words, when He comes and I am in His presence, He is funny! This next descriptive religious experience will exemplify. As I entered Walmart to shop for my groceries, I was sane but I was soon triggered. I started to descend into a psychotic state. As I pushed my shopping cart along things became perceptually very strange and unusual, as is always the case with psychosis. I started to feel out of control and my paranoia grew. But being a pro at psychosis, I continued to mind my own business and to peruse the aisles for my desired goods. As I steamed along, I became increasingly preoccupied. The situation became increasingly dark and characteristically persecutory. I felt like I was the center of attention. My stress level climbed. Then, without forewarning, it happened again.

While of stern deliberation over wheat or rye, another customer entered my proximity and lightning struck yet again. My mind clearly perceived this customer as God personified beyond any sense of doubt. I interacted with God in my customary manner. I said nothing aloud (this would be erratic), but rather engaged in a conversational exchange entirely intrapsychically. Such a characteristic exchange is much like a conversation, but it transacts solely within the confines of my mind.

Before I share God's sense of humor, I want to clarify how this experience would be understood from the clinical perspective. I feel it necessary to parse my craziness for you, my dear reader, as schizophrenia always presents with an inherent type of dualism and/or paradox. From the clinical perspective, the generalized experience would be characterized by "psychosis." The generalized psychosis could then be further deconstructed into its primary constituents. The psychosis would be characterized by "delusions marked by religiosity." The conversation with God is nothing more than the presence of "auditory hallucinations." The entire experience was "triggered" by "feelings of paranoia." This would be the clinical speak to such an experience. And I both understand and value the clinical point of view, but I confess it feels awfully real and truth-based upon its experience! Now with the clinical framework and jargon established, let us get to God's most understated sense of humor!

So, ever so casually, God saunters into my proximity ostensibly for a brief word with my now most attentive but highly troubled mind. My perceptions indicate that here I stand next to the Almighty God, The Supreme Being, The Maker of Heaven and Earth, all omnipotent and omniscient, and the Creator and sustainer of all. Now one may think that this may be perhaps a bit intimidating or perhaps fearfully evocative. But in my experience these exchanges offer no such variables. Rather, the comical often ensues. Now, this is not verbatim as I was absent of pen and paper, but God said to me of the like. "Is it not it humorous, Robert, that we meet in the bread aisle as you have all this psychosis and persecutory feelings going on and all the while you are simply trying to decide between wheat and rye?" Now, I do not know if you find this specified macro/micro juxtaposed situation amusing, but God always knows how to strike the right comic chord with me. Am I alone in thinking God personified speaking to me in the bread aisle as an ordinary humdrum walk-of-life Walmart customer as patently hysterical? Is not God way too important to meet me in the bread aisle at Walmart? Or alternatively, is such a presence divinely touching and somewhat sensible? Perhaps God is presenting Himself in a manner I can accept and interact with beyond any pomp and circumstance. After all, if God presented as the Almighty that He is, and not in a personified manner, having an ordinary conversation might be a bit intimidating. This being the case, if He indeed wanted to help and converse with me, why not in the bread aisle in Walmart? Is there not an intriguing backwards logic to it all? In this typical radical juxtaposition of God and me chatting in Walmart, it takes on such an amusing timbre that it is just too hysterical for containment. And if you are curious, my dear reader, God in fact did cure me of my psychotic ills, because in the end I realized He was most right. I was simply shopping for bread. And by the way, I chose the rye like I always do! Consequently, it follows, I suppose, that I choose both God and rye as my Daily Breads (and in that proper order).

During these hysterical exchanges I have with God, I am acutely aware of the radical juxtaposition of His personified presence. Oftentimes, I find myself smiling and on the verge of outright laughter. But nay, this I know I cannot do! Laughing inappropriately is a known irrational and erratic behavior and a clear tip to psychosis. In these instances, I try to inhibit my laughter, but I must say God really knows how to tickle my funny bone. These comic exchanges always make me wonder why a Divine sense of humor is never discussed in any catechisms, masses, or even in the Bible. After all, why would God not have a sense of humor? Given His omnipotence, He is certainly capable of a knock-knock joke, a pithy riddle, or an amusing anecdote, is He not? I remain perplexed regarding this generalized omission. I once posted on Facebook the query "does God have a sense of humor" and a friend responded with "of course he does, just take a look at the platypus (an egg-laying, duck-billed mammal, i.e., nature's most amusing anomaly)." Touché Steve, touché!

To mix things up I suppose, God does not exclusively present to me in a persistently comic manner. Other times it is as a soothing reassurance. I have had experiences when nearing my utter breaking point of asking myself why I am being so unduly persecuted. God, at times, has responded by means of my auditory hallucinations. I hear God's voice and He indicates that there is a purpose to it all and He reassures me I am plenty strong to endure any such trial. Every time I have these experiences, they are very real to me. As sure as one reads these words, or walks to the mailbox, or eats one's lunch, these experiences are just as real and believable to my perceptive faculties as the otherwise routine and mundane. Such experiences are sublime and each in their own manners and ways. So, I ask myself yet again, is it possible?

The totality of my psychological content includes both the rational and the psychotic. So how does this dualism affect my personal beliefs and perspectives? Certainly, psychotic experiences do not mesh well with the greater shared reality but nevertheless the experiences are real to my personal reality. Clinically speaking, the psychotic experiences are not "real," but what does this invoke? I, too, can discount psychotic experiences as just apparitions, hallucinations, false beliefs, and undue paranoia. But did they in fact occur? Of course they occurred and additionally they were experienced. This dualistic psychology has persisted in my life over considerable time and I have had my recourse to process, reflect, and even conclude on some very pertinent and consequential matters. Therefore, I query, what is in fact real to me based on the totality of all my personal experiences?

16

In Search of Reality

What is real, I ask? In my search to lay firm finger on the pulse of reality, I must first resolve my inherent psychological duality. This dualism, of course, is contained in the opposing polarities of rationality versus psychosis. By contrast, each pole directs to unique metaphysical conclusion. Ostensibly, a diametric prevails, but yet I find these perspectives to remain wholly reconcilable. How might this be so?

Much akin to Zen philosophy, I commonly perceive reality in paradoxical terms. A paradox is like a riddle that has no ostensible solution. But at the same time, I offer that when lost in paradox or wise riddle, the exit to this form of tautological logic can only be achieved by the recognizance of the transcendental ideal. It is only the transcendental that can solve prima facie dualistic riddles and tautologies. Therefore, what is the revelatory transcendental ideal to the spectral rational-psychotic metaphysical paradox?

I begin my search for the **transcendental metaphysical ideal** with the premise of an absolute dubiousness. In pursuit of an epistemology proceeding from the unknown to the known is a most prudent methodology. Certainly, this is not the most settled of bedrock for instigation but worry not- firm foundation is soon to follow. My only access to "reality" comes via an unrelenting series of personal experiences that present to both my mind and body. Labeling certain experiences as "real because rational" and others as "unreal because psychotic" may make sense superficially, but I find this but an oversimplified cognitive veneer lacking in a thorough intellectual cohesion. For I proffer, how is one able to have personal experiences and then by a methodological sleight of hand to characteristically negate them in total as unreal, or as not experienced?

Embedded in my paradoxical psychology, I find a most pertinent distinction. Logical distinctions are a useful means when deconstructing a paradox. Distinctions delineate, or in other words, they indicate the presence of two variables rather than one. It is the equivalent of the logical catchphrase "two and not one." Within my psychology, I see a distinction, and it is evident in the delineation of the "clinical realm" versus the "personal realm." From the clinical perspective, psychotic experiences can be discounted per se because they are otherwise out of step with the macro shared reality. This is most rational and wise in its ways and I too can mitigate certain experiences by manner of inclusion to the greater realm of a psychological pathology or of a cognitive psychosis. Some twenty plus years into schizophrenia, I am aware my psychotic experiences do not mesh well with shared reality. Nevertheless, discarding certain personal experiences in toto both nauseates my stomach and pangs my intellect. I can accept that my gestalt includes psychosis but simply categorizing these experiences as "not real" hinders much more than it assists. Therefore, I have simply chosen the total. There simply is no reason to have to choose between the rational and the psychotic. This is not an either/or paradigm. It is a both/and paradigm. And from this both/and perspective comes my derivative worldviews, beliefs, and especially my empathies. Just as sure as all individuals construct their own personal worldviews based on the totality of their own experiences, I too do the same. And with this inclusive perspective regarding the totality of my experiences comes serene mind along with a sense of holistic health.

I return to the pertinent question of what is "real." In this consideration, I instinctively return to the philosophical luminary René Descartes. Descartes was an intellectual genius and is famously known for esteemed philosophical methodology. Descartes's methodology was the process of continually doubting all he experienced until he reached a premise he could not doubt and de facto established a tautological self-evident truth. After shedding doubt on all his experiences and sensory manifestations, he arrived at his foundational truth, that being "I think, I am." Ultimately, Descartes could not doubt his own thoughts or his own thinking. Descartes believed his premised "I think, I am" was the necessary evidence in proof of his personal existence beyond any sense of a personal doubt. And with existence established betrothed his ensuing complex philosophies.

Descartes's philosophy, like all great and breakthrough theories or ideas, was readily dissected by his contemporaries and by future philosophers to follow.

And while greatly respected and contributory to the philosophical annals of excellence, Descartes's philosophy was ultimately mitigated and reduced to the critical term known as "Cartesian Dualism." This pithy philosophical idiom is the established critical construct to Descartes's philosophy. Philosophers are notoriously known to be meticulously critical. No word or deed will pass by a thoughtful philosopher without serious objection or critique. In philosophy, one offers posits, perhaps even in a manner of pure genius, and then with a focused gaze the rest will critique to find the perceived theoretical faults and vital deficiencies. Alas, I too am now resigned to this very petulant process. Such a methodology is best known by the vernacular moniker of "critical thinking" (which also happens to be the often unstated goal of formalized education).

Criticisms and flaws aside, works of genius are transcendent. The greatest of works rest assuredly on merit and temporally persist with a singular resonance. I must add in a most tangential manner and in avoidance of a dull mechanism, I have always admired genius in all its forms. If I had yet a single narcissistic wish it would be the gift of genius in any of its forms. Oftentimes, genius is accompanied by great personal faults. Perhaps an arrogance, or perhaps a lack of being well-rounded in lieu if one's topical genius. Descartes was a philosophical and literary genius. For all students of philosophy, he remains a mandatory read. Descartes's intellectual genius has even seeped into our modern pop society and can be recognized by the colloquial of "I think, therefore I am." The phrase is often used vernacularly in the context of a solemn joke. Interestingly, the "therefore" was never part of Descartes original premise and should be absent altogether from the pop colloquialism but that is of another topic altogether. Genius has always been intensely fascinating to me. I am not sure as to why, but such it is, and Descartes was a genius. Descartes's writing and thought is rich in original ideas with extraordinary leaps of intuition. If one reads but beyond a few pages of his literature, I think one would quickly discern he was unquestionably of a most sublime form of pure genius.

The moniker of "Cartesian Dualism" is the generalized critical construct to Descartes's philosophy. The primary criticism of his philosophy was that he separated, or caused a duality, between one's mind and one's body. He posited a split rather than the more accepted modern-day notion of the integrated, holistic mind-body perspective. The critical response to Descartes was that his philosophy divided the world into objective mind and its inherent subjects. His critics felt ultimately that his dualism was not entirely accurate. Nevertheless, I, too, think of things dualistically at times- mind primary and all else tertiary. This is the essence of Cartesian thought.

The Cartesian methodology was to systematically doubt all things in all realms until finding the indubitable. Through this doubting process, Descartes ultimately concluded he could not doubt the presence of his own thinking and therefore he offered his postulate of "I think, I am." This Cartesian first premise has a most intriguing correlation to my issues with thought, i.e., psychosis. Contrary to Descartes, I have a diametric sort of personal experience that renders my thought content as highly dubitable. Delusions, constituted by groupings or sets of related thoughts, are clinically conceived as "not real." Psychosis, by definition, indicates that which one is thinking is not part of what is considered "real." Descartes asserted the correlation of thoughts and "reality" while my experiences with psychosis indicate thoughts and "not reality." When psychotic, my thoughts do not correspond well with the larger reality. Contrary to Descartes, dubiousness reigns rampant in my thought content. Due to experiential episodes with psychosis, I can cast doubt on all things including thought primary. My generalized sense of reality is but a blurred abstraction drenched in an essential and persistent dubiousness. I doubt my thoughts, my existence, the existence of the others, the trees in the forest, the sun in the sky, and even our specious humanity (in all its absurdity). But this characteristic type of thinking is not of any matter not yet approached. Such thinking is simply a categorical form of extreme "philosophical skepticism."

Assertions of a most thorough dubiousness are contained in the auspices of the philosophic realms known as "skepticism" or "extreme skepticism." Skepticism becomes the doubting of all, or in other words, as knowing nothing to be true, factual, or even existent. The criticism of skepticism is that as a theory it draws no conclusions beyond the assertion of a prevailing dubiousness. Additionally, skepticism fails as a coherent theory due to a covert but inherent logical implosion. If one believes all is dubious then de facto dubiousness becomes a known certainty. This certainty is the logical fallacy inherent to the theory of skepticism that asserts no certainties. I also consider skepticism a timid philosophy in that in its purest form it inherently posits no essential first truth or no first self-evident premise. Absent of a first premise, no logically coherent theory of any type or characteristic can follow. Skepticism therefore falls short of prominence due to its inherent logical fallacy and more importantly due to its lack of conviction in an established first truth. In my search for metaphysical reality and truth, therefore, I must abandon both Descartes and skepticism and proceed with view to other horizons.

Admittedly, I am most skeptical regarding assertions of known absolutes or certainties. I often view life as highly arbitrary and characteristically relativistic.

I can doubt this and that ad infinitum. I cast aspersions on assertions of known quantities or stated universals. I am a skeptic in this sense. But along with this skeptical and critical disposition comes the contrary trait of a most profound abiding belief in the value of personal conviction. This contrary juxtaposition is reconciled by the both/and paradigmatic quantum perspective and I find no logical flaw in the diametric viewpoints. Well-guided personal convictions are an absolute bedrock and persistent conduit to an abiding human morality. Humanity's conglomerate of perseverative convictions forges, maintains, and ultimately refines our integral moralities. Humanity's most Ideal convictions facilitate that which is inherently good, just, and most civilized. Absent of the conviction ideal the moral societal ties that bind dissipate and atrocities and incivilities become the consequent derivatives.

I often feel at a crossroads of what is real and what is not, and this of course is due to the inherent ambiguities that come with psychosis. At one time, psychosis shoved me into an existential corner by manner of novel paradoxes strewn with complexities. But given the grace of familiarity, I have learned and I have solved, at least in measure to sustain. My solution belies in the recognizance of the transcendental ideal. It is the transcendent ideal that now keeps my gaze rather the paradoxical riddle (psychosis). I must confess I have grown most weary of the "this is real and this is not" psychological paradigm that has permeated my life for so many years. So instead, I allow paradox one to be paradox one, then simply attach to its corresponding ideal. I think it correlates well with **Plato's idea of the cave.** It is nothing more than a search for light in darkness, and with good result.

I often think when I pass away, the ultimate truth or truths will be revealed. I view death as a genesis rather than a fete de complete. And if death is not the end but yet a new beginning, what characteristic follows? I suppose you and I will ultimately discover. In the meanwhile, a meditative foci on transcendent ideals has become a typical salve and thus a worthy occupation. And in lieu of a well-crafted literary foreshadowing, my dear reader, I simply offer God as the ultimate alpha-omega transcendental ideal.

Once mired in the details of life, my existential focus has shifted to the "big picture." Admittedly, I have developed an apathy regarding the "dailiness" of life. In many ways, yesterday resembles today both in thought and experience. And tomorrow will resemble today as today did yesterday. Life is no doubt repetitive. Add to this life inherency human habit, and one giant spin-cycle results. Why brush your teeth in a different manner everyday when the most efficient manner has already been established? Habits promote efficient living. Regularity and habituation, therefore, are integral to our lives. I amusingly label this global phenomenon an exalted form of "existential scurry." But personally, I am trying to gracefully disengage. By the same accord, however, comes the prima facie acknowledgement that the dailiness of life is embedded by trait. For what else is there to do but to scurry? Well, I offer to you, my dear reader, that just beyond this paradoxical scurry belies the paramount transcendent ideal…and you won't be disappointed.

17

The Sacred and The Profane

My dear reader, I must inform, I have found my metaphysical grail, and my reality has been claimed. Psychosis has backfired in its intent of disturbance, confusion, and entropy. Rather, in a most causal manner, psychotic affliction has led to metaphysical clarity. From chaos has come order. Psychosis persists by paradox and dualism, but I have found the answerable by form ideal. I have reached my metaphysical crest, and therein stands the grail. Embolden on its urn reads, "truth characteristically resides in **the sacred and the profane**."

The spectral items of the sacred and the profane both oppose as ideals and contrast as corollaries. But I truncate, please do not misconstrue and attach the ostensible value judgments to each. They both must abide, in necessary contrast. For only from one can come the other,

Firstly, I must clarify, it is from my specified personal experience that come my metaphysical conclusions. Characteristically, therefore, I am concluding matters by means of an intuitive logic. As such, my derivative assertions rest solely as hypotheses and with no allusions of proffered fact. Nevertheless, we all have our personal inclinations and intuitions, and such specificities are the essential politic to our inherency. And when we behave by virtue respect, latitudes for opinion and perspective prevail. And when we do not, pugilists thrive.

I conclude that most of all human experience, both yours and mine, can be definitively categorized within the confines of the profane ideal. The essence and primary constitution of the profane ideal is revealed and experienced by manner and form of human "suffering." In the end, and all things considered, suffering is the true metaphysics. I suppose I fall in line behind **Buddha** on this matter, however distant I may be in queue. Simply stated, when one suffers, life matters. And when life matters, a sense of reality absorbs into our mind and soul. "Welcome to reality," a personified sufferance will exclaim, "is this real enough for you?" More than any other characteristic type of experience, including the contrasting extremes of elation or euphoria, the most "real" experiences humanity endures and frequents are by manner and process of personal suffering. No one opts to suffer unnecessarily or to suffer if there are other options available, yet suffering prevails. Suffering obtrusively places "reality" at your doorstep. Life becomes most "real" when we are in pain and when we are suffering.

I often think "there but for the grace of God, go I." With such a typical leaning comes empathy. By trait, most people are empathic and are willing to help others when possible (individual capacitation for empathy is a paramount psychological consideration, but this is of another matter). Of course, we also want the best for ourselves, including being free of any untenable suffering. The experience of suffering resides on a tolerability spectrum. Some forms are unconscionable, abhorrent, and evil by wreckage; others, more subtle, blunt, and delicate by delivery. Beguilingly, its levy comes in no fair ratio, while its source is an incalculable whole. Some suffer from happenstance, certain diseases for example, while others endure from the deliberate and neglect hands of our own. In total, suffering exudes. Its restoration is a fountainhead; its characteristic, inventive.

I find suffering and reality inseparable. The two are so tightly fused that distinction is but a misnomer. With suffering comes life with texture, or distinct feel. We all seemingly wait in abeyance until our number is called and our lot delivered. Afflictions of war, disease, abuse, famine, tyranny, poverty, and crime are all too familiar to the human psyche. Eventually, all come to bear. And with life duration, most oft develops a dispositional acquiescence. Suffering is the true metaphysics. It universally abounds and reverberates. And the remains? Yet unaffected scurry.

It is only by an ample course of grace am I afforded the luxury of philosophic meandering. Many have no such luxury due to interminable conditions of suffering. Make no mistake, my diatribes are of overflow and luxury. I am most fortunate to be able to write in such convenience. While I sit in comfort and pen, others are held hostile by grips of malady and malaise. "There but for the grace of God, go I." I find this Biblical phrase often attributable.

Admittedly, suffering is a formidable foe. Its action of mechanism is wily. If not somatic, then psychological; if not personally, then by proxy. But of what characteristic is the suffering generic? Does suffering come with existential meaning? And if so, can it extend in relevance beyond its own parameters? The answer to these are "yes." Existential suffering is present with reason and permeates with cause. Suffering is the yin to our yang. In other words, it only exists by contrast. It does not exist in isolation, or in a metaphysical vacuum. As such, like all existential considerations, suffering too comes with associated corollaries.

When absent of poignant travail, I exhale and appreciate. I have learned by course of affliction that life offers no guarantees. I view the future as but a proliferated form of possibility, rather than a bankable sort of certainty. Today's quantifiable universally wanes to a status null, and tomorrow follows only on predicates of possibility. For those amid darkness, in any of its forms, I empathize. If in proximity, I offer hand.

My hope for all is a substantive temporal salve followed by a most sublime eternal salvation. I find these to be the matters of significance nay yet the details. These are the cresting mountains upon which I maintain my steady gaze. So, as I scurry about in the luxury of deciphering metaphysical truisms, others are suffering. To those in sufferance, reality belies far beyond any matters of existential quibble. Rather, reality is concrete, harsh, and perhaps even nauseating. I shudder at the sufferings of others. I find it to be a most harsh world sometimes, but admittedly, I have acquiesced. If it is reality you seek, I direct to the eager eyes of those who suffer, and there it will be found. From suffering eyes you will see.

I have had my ration of suffering. My lot happens to be psychological. Delusions of persecution cause me the most anguish. Specifically, perceptions involving eternal damnation are the most provocative. But thankfully, these perceptions remain transient and as such my suffering defaults to a bearance.

There is a relativism to the generic of suffering. For example, my father had brain cancer and died at age forty-one. He endured seven brain operations over the course of two most trying years. The cancer ravaged his body but found no port to his soul. Towards the end of his life, his ordeal included deformity, blindness, aphasia, and paralysis. But despite his condition (and when still ably vocal), his shared mantra was "things could always be worse." He did not complain or self-pity. He was adaptively idyllic over the course of his literal and figurative malignancy. "It could always be worse," he would say. My father capably repelled his malady, and in doing so, he remained integral; that is, within the bounds of his soul. His attitude made it easier on those around him to cope with his obvious and incremental decline. Given such a trying lot, his psychology was remarkable. Both well and ill, he was an inspiration. I still miss him today.

I often think my father's mantra, "things could always be worse," and how it applies to suffering, in the generic. In his sentiment, I find a paradoxical truism. Side one, a sober and grave commentary; side two, an embedded optimism. Next, by manner of its phrasing, when one side prevails, the other embeds; and when one embeds, the other prevails. Both sides are distinct, yet whole. Reframed in the vernacular, therefore, comes "despite suffering, sustenance remains," i.e., for if things could worsen, a quality must yet abide. By accordance, this paradox deconstructs, but only to quickly reabsorb. But from its inherency, I again see the embedded value characteristic to the quality of suffering.

Can a single ray of sunshine illume an entire forest? In the movie ***The Shawshank Redemption***, a film I hold in a most high esteem, the motif of hope is expansively explored. The main character and protagonist, Andy, is a duly man wrongly convicted of murder and incarcerated to a life sentence. After decades of wrongful incarceration, he successfully executes his meticulous escape from the prison (Shawshank) and subsequently reclaims his freedom on an idyllic, boundaryless Mexican beach. Andy leaves in his wake a letter to his good friend and fellow inmate Red. The two had previously talked about "hope" on a few separate occasions. Red found no value in hope, but Andy was much the different. In the letter Andy writes, "always remember, Red, hope is a good thing, perhaps the best of things." Throughout his ordeal, Andy maintained a lighted hope during his otherwise dark and unjust sufferance. Hope was Andy's sustenance.

Hope flickers to the ailing mind. It is an intangible sensibility, with tangible efficacy. When conditions are dark and troubled, hope often stands alone in opposition. When in ample supply, hope protects and solaces. Victor Frankl, in his classic book ***Man's Search for Meaning***, writes of his survival as a prisoner in a Nazi concentration camp. Frankl explains how he found sustenance amid his suffering. During the most evil and inhumane conditions, Frankl writes of his epiphany regarding the human capacitation for attitudinal choice. The tidy maintenance of managing one's attitude may sound highly generic and banal, but this is only so because of Frankl's prologue. Frankl's ideas contained in *Man's Search for Meaning* became the instigate to a canon now known as "**positive psychology.**" And since the time of Frankl's introduction, no less than a massive inundation has ensued on the topic of attitudinal countenance. While encamped, Frankl correlates his hopeful attitude with his ultimate survival. He underlines a meaningful semiotic amid the otherwise inhumane. In one anecdote, Frankl details a derivative joy from sharing his petty rationed bread with a commiserate and friend. In this, he found his meaning. In this, he found his sustenance.

Amid suffering, hope pools. No one is exempt, however, from its occasional loss. Hope eludes my disposition, at times, but it again reveals and restores. From its stream, I am sustained. I find the adage, "hope springs eternal," both sublime and wise. It indeed is a wellspring, and its supply interminable; its ration, however, can be stubborn and elusive. At times, hope's accessibility requires deliberation. But once it flows, hope pierces the dark with castings of light, like no other agent. And from its brilliance sight restores, the profane folds, and the sacred reveals.

18

The Sacred Ideal

Hope parses suffering. In addition to hope comes the divine as sourceful sustenance. When situations are too great for one's own power and will some turn to their faith and to their belief in the divine, or in God. Surely, not all turn to God either when troubled or when well. Faith in God is a personal choice.

Some believe according to the primary religions. Others are more scientific in their proclivities and may conceive of God more in terms of an energy or **chi** of sorts. Still others, through meditative practices may think of humanity's oneness as a God form or may view enlightenment as divinity. Such stratified ascertains and gilded notions default de facto as individual-centric, and in many ways, each seemingly approaches God in a particularized manner based on personal inclinations. In other words, in pertinence of the divine, coherent uniformity is lacking (although not entirely). And of course, any such personal belief also presents on a qualitative spectrum with capacitation for proximate waxing and waning. As such, proclamations of a personal "faith" are best understood as a psychological construct with available, and often opportune, variation.

Certainly not all proclaim a belief in God. Some vow atheism or perhaps a form of humanism. Such inclinations, similarly to the tenets of the faith-based, also customarily carry expectations for idyllic moral standards and derivative human conduct. Although atheists and humanists disavow "God," usually such individuals nevertheless maintain their personal metaphysical presumptions similarly to those of the faiths. And when one has a metaphysical inclination or conclusion, it follows de facto that said individuals have beliefs pertaining to the metaphysical whole (or totality). In other words, each maintains their sense of a constituent reality. Although God per se is disavowed, when one has convictions pertaining to the whole, then "reality" again emerges as a transcendent idea or conceptualization. In this sense, both those of the faiths and those exempt similarly have beliefs about an existential superlative that transcends the singular existential experience. Put in another manner, both maintain the whole as constitutionally greater than the sum of its parts. It follows, therefore, when directly addressing that of the existential whole the concept of "divinity" again emerges as an existential superlative, although not necessarily by form of "God" per se. With this, the distinctive lines are drawn between that of "God" and the "divine" and that of the "religious" and the "secular."

I find It interesting that individuals often take great comfort in being around others with beliefs similar to their own. Such phenomena is culturally pervasive, and its dynamic comes with sociological intrigue. I suppose it is conciliatory. It reinforces beliefs and reassures convictions. Its presence can be seen in "siloed" religious denominations absent of creed admixture. Worship is unified, and dissenters congregate of their own. Similarly to religious congregation, like-minded congregation can also be found in political systems. Red versus blue, for example. Personally, I am no fan of siloed intellectualism and I harbor no qualms in opposing perspective. In fact, I find consolation in intellectual dissent, for only by opposition eventually yields the transcendent, or the idyllic. Inherently, transcendence is that which overcomes dualism, or a stark opposition, that otherwise appears irreconcilable. This I have discovered via my trials with schizophrenia. Without recognition of transcendentals, I would be perpetually marooned in an unresolvable paradox. Oppositional dualism is nicely exemplified in the marital fete de complete of "irreconcilable differences." I find this term a most comical misnomer and I often chuckle at its intonation when in ear-bent. I suppose marriage is exclusive to the generalized laws of the universe and I wager in a most sturdy manner! So much for "we will have to agree to disagree!" Just sign the papers dammit (remember, my dear reader, humor is golden!).

I have admiration for intellectual intermingling. Such can be found in typical interfaith centers of worship and in religious services of inclusion found in certain community institutions. I also find an aesthetic in the political of "crossing party lines" when of proper conviction. Humanity's everlasting peace will never be constructed on a theoretical unilateralism but rather only on divergent yet harmonious discord. I find it most vital to share company with others not of like-mindedness and of differing perspectives. Respect for differences of opinion is cliché but it brings heavy bearence. Many have no such tolerance. Some engage in pugilism for sport, and consequently, harmonious discord is evasive and rests as an unlearned behavior. And so, humanity fights and it wars. For some, world peace is not just some idealized juvenile notion and it seems readily achievable. Living a peaceful life really is not all too complicated but it is often confoundingly conceived as some typified "**Goldbergian**" mechanism. Peace is available for the taking. I see it clearly, my dear reader. Contrarians, I suppose, are of the inclination that he who bangs the table most forcibly, wins. And so, it churns. The Lilliputians dispute and the strife persists. Such is characteristic of the idyllic profane.

The question of God has been debated since man's arrival and will continue to be a topic of much contention. With human diversity comes creed diversity. Not all are of the same religious bent. For some, theology feverishly courses the veins, and approaches psychological frenzy. Add to this inherency the ingredient of ideational dissent, and remarkably humanity finds reproach in self-inflicted crusades and brotherly call to arms. As history will attest, all too often war finds its etiology in frenetic religiosity. With such outcomes, poles transpose and glorified ends pervert to violent means. Or, in other words, from human corruption follows the profanity of war.

Profanity never sources from the sacred proper. It is an impossibility, in the most strict sense. Rather, it is from sacrilege that comes the profane. Humans by nature are inherently prone to psychological distortion. With such distortions, ideals obfuscate. But despite our pedestrian means, the sanctity of the ideal remains, both unaffected and coherent. Only from distortion comes profanity, and its acrimony. The sacred idyllic persists immutable. It was, is, and will always be.

19

"I Conclude, God"

I have had my ration of religious experiences. These, I reference, are my discrete perceptions of en vivo interactions with God. I do not seek such experiences, but yet they occur. I can attribute my religiosity as psychosis, conjured. Or, I can conclude otherwise, or of some combination. I must warrant, I find "God" the paramount personal matter, beyond any other. Individual beliefs abound, and on a most broad spectrum ranging from devout to non-belief. Some affirm, others deny; some assured, others skeptical. I have no qualms of dissent. I simply find God a most personal matter with availing choice for each.

Only from choice comes human freedom. Autonomy is the push-back to coercion and oppression. As such, freedom is characteristic of the sacred, while oppression the profane. Capacity for choice is no small matter. It carries massive existential significance, specifically the spectral freedom/bondage tangibility. When individual autonomy routinely subjugates to the motivations of a collectivity, societal bondage follows. This is the essence of oppression.

I find a most aesthetic beauty in the exercise of moral free will. Perhaps this is why I am most comfortable with intellectual dissent. I welcome all perspectives, if not a too heavy form of psychological distortion, or pathology. And so, it is with my capacity for choice that I offer my derivative conclusions and convictions pertaining to God.

In the exercise of personal choice, my dear reader, my attestation has arrived and comes by form and phrase, "I conclude, God." From this intuitive end comes my derivative beliefs and convictions. And for purposes of a bona fide clarity, I offer my religious tenets (in degree). My God is the God of Catholicism. God is

Almighty. His son is Divine Jesus. Divine essence is that of the Holy Spirit. These are the integral constituents. Within my faith, figures of sanctity abound. I lend credence to the Virgin Mary, apostles, saints, prominent disciples, and the Holy Pope. Over the temporal course of Catholicism, key personages have emerged and in varying degrees of relevance and providence. The faith stays meticulous in its tracking of prominent figures and historical lineages.

I believe in the Word of the Lord as contained in The Holy Bible, and as written by His chosen people. Within its contents, The Bible includes literal, figurative, and allegorical regale. It is purely nonfiction, rather creative. In its narrative, The Bible details the historical progression of the faith. The Bible begins at Genesis 1:1, which reads "In the beginning God created the heaven and the earth" and ends chronologically around A.D. 95 with the final book entitled "Revelations." As entity, The Bible is a complex and multifactorial semiotic.

I offer a few last items of relevance, concerning The Bible. The Bible is chronologically linear. It is sophisticated, by detail. These qualities lend to its cogency. Within its contents, The Bible offers commentary on moral code, and I suggest of a lasting legacy. Certain logistical matters are addressed including inception, development, and maintenance of the church. Proper worship is explicated, including intention and ceremonial form. And lastly, after reading The Bible, attendance at a present-day Catholic mass comes with an unforeseen sensibility. It took considerable time to read, but I did complete. For a variety of reasons, it was the most important read of my life, and this comes with easy declaration.

During psychosis, I have had personal exchanges with God. These are sublime. The absolution, of course, is the qualifier "during psychosis." Only by its predication follows such particularity. Therefore, given such an inherency, paradox again reveals. I must decide, for the betterment of my mental health, the dispositional breach. In regard to these experiences, is psychological elimination best, or psychological integration? Better to mitigate or resound? This matter has plagued me for many years, twenty in the least. But, with such a duration, also has come some clarity.

Regarding my religiosity and its related paradox, I am impelled to first discuss what I believe to be one of the greatest of all ideas. The idea is sourced from the Danish philosopher Soren Kierkegaard (1813-1855). Kierkegaard was a most astute philosopher and theologian and his intellectual canon is historically bound in legend. Kierkegaard was an influential advocate of Catholicism and his writings are contributory to the faiths generalized catechisms. Kierkegaard is most prominently known for his idea of "a leap of faith." The phrasing "a leap of faith" has become a modern euphemism and its etiology comes directly from Kierkegaard. In the phrasings banality, Kierkegaard's brilliance reverberates. Kierkegaard philosophized that one could never "know with certainty" whether or not God existed. From a philosopher's perspective, knowing with certainty equates to "knowledge" and is descriptive of matters beyond the ordinary vernacular. Of the three canons of philosophy, the exploration of matters pertaining to the "known" is referred to as epistemology. Over the course of the history of philosophy, many have offered hypotheses pertaining to that which is known. To this current day, however, no such theory remains undisputed. Knowledge per se is a most serious consideration to a philosopher and its standard is of the highest order. Kierkegaard was well aware of the superlative requisites to a theoretical knowledge. So, by form of his specified genius, Kierkegaard surreptitiously argued that because of knowledge absent, the question of God's existence could never be rectified of the human standards of epistemological knowledge. Kierkegaard thought of God's existence as otherworldly and beyond the acumen and capacity of human reason. On these premises followed his catechisms.

Many great minds have come and gone, but theological certainty remains wholly unsubstantiated. From the confines of human reason, the proof of God's existence remains both elusive and enigmatic. Perhaps the subjectivity of human reason is minuscule; that is, when chasing the divine. Another intellectual legend, of some noted repute, is that of the most singular Albert Einstein. Einstein is famous for his desire, above all else, to know the mind of God. This was Einstein's most coveted grail, and much of his metaphysics reflected this quest. Einstein was pure mathematical genius, and through his mathematics he revealed many truths concerning the properties of the physical universe. He was enchanted by the mathematical exactness to the universal churn. In this exactness, he was convinced of intelligent design, and de facto, of an ultimate Creator, or God. Einstein's metaphysical genius remains unmatched to this day. He was revelatory and revolutionary. But he too, like Kierkegaard and multitudes, ultimately could not break the evidentiary code to parlay the existence of God. Therefore, to this very moment, the grail sustains.

By means of rational deduction, I conclude God's proven existence as irretrievable. All such efforts, forlorn. If Kierkegaard and Einstein fall short, what further recourse is had? After all, these are two of the best hitters in our lineup (a baseball reference, my dear reader, lest we forget our sensibility for levity). Mankind's deductive reasoning, while prolific in its scientific and technological advancement, seemingly cannot get beyond itself in revelation to the existence of God. The scientific often approaches divine graces, but yet does not reach. With this may come a sense of despair, especially for those seeking the evidentiary. Such an inherency, however, provokes me no ail; for by manner circumstantial, recourse avails. And per chance, it too comes with a formative abidance to reason.

The heretofore established laws of the universe exude mathematical exactness. Given such precision, science customarily inclines to the hypothesis of intelligent design. With this typical leaning, science has been revelatory in petitions of worldly order, but its sourcing comes void of cogitable trace. Science reverberates with numeric orderliness, but its impetus remains wholly obscured. In similitude, it is akin to the referential euphemistic riddle, "**the ghost in the machine**;" as such, the possibility of a creative universe, sourced divine, remains both enigmatic and unqualified.

Man's scientific grail of a "theory of everything" remains questioningly unknown. As such, man's current metaphysical status rests as an unresolved endeavor. A resolute and coherent theory of everything has proven to be chronically and sophisticatedly elusive. Simply stated, man wants to comprehensively understand the universe. Man wants to know "everything," creation and mechanics included. This grail has occupied many theorists from many canons. Some explore the parameters of the universe from a purely scientific lens while others peer from a more ethereal or spiritual lens. But man's metaphysical aspirations will never be fully quenched until "everything" is understood, and coherently explained. And this returns me to God and the matter of Godly existence. For, if God exists, man's grail takes brunt with capacity for metaphysical resolution. At current status, however, God's existence remains at hypothesis. Necessarily, therefore, this is not a negation of God's existence but rather indicates an evidentiary insufficiency for scientific conclusion, or known fact. But again, for me and in pertinence to God, I assert there is yet more to the story!

20

Yet Rational Recourse for the Existence of God

There is a logic and rationality well-known to man of prominent utility but not yet of the gold standard of the deductive processes. This methodology is known as inferential reasoning or inferential logic. For purposes of differentiation, deductive reasoning, briefly stated, proceeds from the known general to the "deduced" known specific. Conversely, inferential reasoning proceeds from the known specific to the "inferred" known general.

When of a vigorous coherence, the deductive lends of certitude and the factual while when of vigor the inferential lends to assertion and hypothesis. The strength of the inferential methodology comes with its allowances for an increased creativity while still remaining within the realm of the rational. Argumentation of an effective inferential persuasion can be the instigate to its further testing via the deductive methodology. And if the once inferential persists in theory beyond the rigors of the deductive processes, then comes the promulgation of scientific certainty and fact. In this capacity, inferential logic is a powerful technology but at the same time comes with the acknowledgment of proof yet to be served.

This preluding banter concerning systemic reasoning now returns me to point and to my query of God's existence. God's existence persistently eludes the deductive manner, including the constructive efforts of humankind's historically brightest and most astute. But I yet wager twofold. Firstly, pertaining to God's existence, I find the inferential as most neglect and erroneously undervalued. Secondly, I posit God's existence as inherently of the inferential realm and characteristically will never be revealed of the deductive processes. With this so stated, the God concept returns for existential consideration by manner of inferential reason and logic, and it does so with a vigor.

Since the inferential methodology inherently flows from the specified to the generalized, it is the singular, or the individual, that situates in theoretical prominence, rather the generalized of the deductive processes. In this context, therefore, personal experience becomes the specification and hence the predicate to the inferential posit. Characteristically, from cogent specification follows "possibility" and from cogent generalization follows "fact." Further, when an intuitive capably generalizes, the once intuitive transmutes to fact. Of course, conversely, when an intuitive fails the general specs, it then sieves as "not fact." When "not fact," by status, the intuitive salvage characteristically and necessarily rests at personal opinion, or personal belief, and not beyond.

From this discussion of logical processes comes the rest (and best) of the story. Given the inferential methodology, a reasonable intuitive meets logical critical standard. It follows, therefore, from the datum of personal experience ensues hypothetical opportunity. Of these, a Godly ontology consumes as opportune. It comes by recognition only by the inheritance of inferential logic that reasonably follow theological assertions, and this is currently without exception. At the same time, any such assertions must associate as an inherent intuitive, and not fact. As such, for some may follow a spiritual deterrence, especially those seeking the deductive evidentiary; but for others, faith prevails, by trait. In the end, God's existence simply becomes a matter of personal perspective

The existence of God has been proffered tenfold by those of the differentiated populous century upon century, and one. I find this most intriguing for the inferential hypothesis of God's existence seemingly will not scatter. It has reverberated through the temporal and resonated across the cultural. Its ideational occupancy is prolific. It is a hypothesis of promulgation without apparent punctuation. Yet it remains but an unproven.

In pertinence of scientific fact and certitude, I caution misnomer. All science, beyond exception, avails disputation. Even the best items of scientific certainty can be cast an existential doubt, if ever so-inclined. There is a tremendous relevancy to our world. Things can be "both this and that," and things can also be "not this and not that." Combinations, as well, may prevail. Ultimately, my dear reader, I find we are all left to our own to conclude for our own. In my instance, this at one time was provocative of angst. Now, however, I find peace by this condition. I can think and believe of my own choosing, and you of yours, and absent of acrimony. In context, therefore, God's existence can rest comfortably with believers, and non-existence comfortably with non-believers.

When considering the existence of God, I first harken to the testimonies of Kierkegaard. Kierkegaard was a stern advocate for the existence of God. But similarly to all those prior, Kierkegaard was unable to prove the existence of God by manner of a coherent scientific methodology. But at the same time, amidst his efforts came a lasting legacy. In pertinence of God's existence, Kierkegaard proffered a profound yet simple epiphytic assertion. Kierkegaard's legacy came with his idea of a necessary "leap of faith."

Kierkegaard's "leap of faith" is an inferential phrasing. It altogether lacks dogma and comes with no generalizable conclusion. In fact, Kierkegaard admitted God's existence was not evidentiary. He acknowledged a base uncertainty. At the same time, however, Kierkegaard squarely believed. So, in support of his position and after much philosophy, he ultimately constructed his ontological sequela. Kierkegaard reasoned inferentially, he predicated "a leap of faith," and he concluded existence.

In addition to the profundity of Kierkegaard's ideational leap, I also find a recursive irony. Regarding inferential reasoning, consider its procedural whole from premise to conclusion. Like most systems, from the crank of the mechanical comes the rotary of execution. In this instance, a reasonable leap becomes the requisite crank to the rotary of intuitive conclusion. In other words, if one is convinced of a matter despite the threshold of evidence, then it necessarily follows that an inherent leap has occurred in one's reasoning, and this is without exception. In this sense, Kierkegaard leapt twice, both in his assertion and by his methodology, and in this I find a satisfying irony.

With my psychosis comes a volatile and unstable sense of reality with an ostensible lack of firm experiential grounding. Add to the equation derivative transactional exchanges with God and my reality-based sensibilities takes further personal brunt. But in response to this dilemma, I have indeed found a sense of a grounded experiential reality although admittedly I had to expand the parameters to my consideration. Therefore, by course of psychotic tribulation and by manner of meditative response, I find my experiences with psychosis to inherently have a most lucid correlate to Kierkegaard's positional assertion of a necessary "leap of faith." And by accordance to his wisdom, I have found a convincing psychological integrity.

I function on faith. I sincerely do and allow me to explain. In my efforts to cope with psychosis, my perceptions indicate "x," but I must behave in manner "y." After all, by trait, my perceptions are psychotic and if I behave concertedly, I end up in right field, turning circles, and picking daisies! So, alternatively, I proceed on faith and act the rational part. I often think to myself that I should be a **SAG** nominee for best actor in a lead role! But it works! Sometimes I lose faith and become sneakily influenced by my psychotic perceptions and during these times I struggle, and I tussle, and I churn. In times of adequate faith, however, my life calms and a subtle aesthetic can emerge. But truth be told, my life only works when I cognitively value the ideational leap and behave according to an abiding faith. Further, all of this requires routine reaffirmation. And so my faith leads, and I follow. And in repose I often reflect, "aaah sweet Kierkegaard...a treasured companion of mine! With you, I too will leap!"

Functioning in this manner is Zen-like. It comes characterized by repeated psychological leaps of faith while otherwise enmeshed in a psychological terror. With each leap comes ample doses of behavioral rationality. This methodology eliminates behavior associative with psychosis. In many ways, making these repeated leaps of faith during an active psychosis is the primary coping means I use to stay in the game of the mutually shared reality. Admittedly, however, this is a skill singularly panned from trial. I only adopted strict dispositional rationality from the lessons of repeated so-called failures. Such an accordance is pragmatic and utilitarian, but it is yet a panacea. Schizophrenia, after all, is a disease and not just a bundle of learned Jedi mind-tricks. So regression occurs, but I try not to fuss. All things considered, acting the rational part sustains, and I find this enough.

As a dovetail to my chronicles of a secular faith, I now offer my lauds of an otherworldly characteristic. As previously mentioned, I am Catholic by denomination. My belief in God abounds, and my doubts are particulate. At times, God's presence in my life has been supportive and at other times persecutory. I find this no matter. I do my best with what He offers, and I surrender the rest to His will. During times of psychosis, I have had perceptively vivid interactions with God, as personified. By choosing, I psychologically integrate these rather than dismiss. I do not conduct by preach or sanctity. I keep my blessings and tidings from God securely nested between my own two ears. I do not magnify my Divine ideations. They occur, and I take notice. I do not tread beyond this recognizance. I have an easy ontological acceptance, approaching casualness. Our relationship is simple, enduring, and ordinary. I trust God's will and plan, and the rest I consider the details.

God, or not God, is decisional. Its tipping-scale ought derive from an essential liberty rather provoked from pushy influence, or even coercion. Of your choosing, I have no qualms. I find God a supremely personal issue and best left for each to decide. In the end, however, when all ontological frenzy and histrionic are cast and decision appeals, one either takes the leap or one does not. I, for one, have taken the leap.

The corollary to the leap of faith of course is its qualitative destination. So, I proffer, what is the quality of faith? Firstly, as defined, I find "faith" synonymous to "a belief without doubt;" or, otherwise stated, belief minor doubt, equates faith. Given the astutely skeptical nature of the human mind, however, such a measure becomes a difficult proposition. In a phenomenological sense, by capacity, faith prevails as anomaly. Further, if once attained comes no bearance to perpetuity. Ample today may be bereft tomorrow. And when in pertinence to the mystified Divine, faith by characteristic can be a most reticent sort of creature.

A favorite story of mine from the Bible paints an illustrative picture of the nuance of "faith gained, faith lost." God's given son, Jesus, leaves the company of his apostles for reasons of solitude. The apostles notice he has left and travel to seek him. Several take a boat across the water in His search. When they find Jesus, an apostle stands to address Christ from the boat. Christ tells the apostle to come hither to me by manner of steps on the water. The apostle states it is impossible to do so, but Jesus responds with reiteration. The apostle starts out from the boat and takes several capable steps on the water before then plunging to its depths. The apostle retorts Jesus of the adverse occurrence. Christ replies to the apostle that he lost his faith in the word of God. Jesus asks the apostle, "why did you doubt" this capacity? Jesus goes on to explain that while in the state of faith the apostle ably walked on water, as directed. But when he lost his faith in the Word, and his doubt arose, he then submerged. I find this an impeccable story of the psychological polarities of faith. When ample in faith, capacity ensued. But when negligent, came reproach. And such it is when the unduly seeds of doubt are sown to the often fickle mind.

With my psychosis comes the sacred and profane, as actuated phenomena. The sacred entails sublime religiosity characterized by abundant faith. Such experiences are indelible. The profane exudes by a wickedness, as only psychosis can render. Such experiences, too, are indelible. Given these polarities, I therefore return full circle to my cognitive occupation of what is "real" and what is "not real." From such an experiential wake, a reconciliation begs. And after a long psychic journey of a felt centurion duration, a cognitive truce has been met, and a conciliation bartered. It comes by form of "a leap of faith" in the direction of the Lord. It comes by graces of gratitude and humility. With such a resolve, I am most at ease.

I find issues of faith to caustically dwell foremost in the hearts and minds of you and me. I am convinced issues of deity are best resolved first in the individual and then perhaps a corresponding community can take esteem and favor. As for me, my convictions have been forged and from this center I leap. And aside from the eminence of God, loved ones, and a circumspect morality, the rest seem as detail. The vagaries of life now portray by the veneer of a temporal lollygag, and with a characteristic sort of pomp and sophistication. This I see as a consequence of priority.

21

Living the Leap

We are fast approaching our ultimate destination of text complete, my dear reader, and I feel an urgent sense of required pith and wisdom. Of these requisites, I will bring my best sporting game! I would like to address a few last pragmatics regarding psychosis. Firstly, despite schizophrenia, I am able work. During psychosis, my effectiveness may erode in the least but I have long ago abandoned any illusions of perfection, so I do not obsess. Additionally, my psychosis now capably obfuscates, so my stress hormones no longer scream. When conquering schizophrenia, obfuscation is an essential. So I have learned some necessary skills and coping means to persist in occupation. It is not always easy, but nor is my askance. I also must reiterate that psychosis does not necessarily equate to violence. I do not want to be a source of any alarm to considerations of workplace safety. Psychosis and violence are distinctly two, and not one. I can assure, in my personhood, I am safe as a Red Sox fan at Fenway.

Psychosis is a livable condition. I think there may be a vernacular misunderstanding and linguistic misnomer with its mention. Psychosis is often correlated with an untenable crazed-state capably prone to violence. I hope I have sufficiently dispelled this myth. Psychosis is not without redemption and temperance. Despite its presence, individuals may work, engage in meaningful relationships, be self-sufficient, and generally take care of their own matters and their own business. Certainly, however, psychosis comes with no ordinations, but nor does life in the general. Nevertheless, an ample and healthy sustenance is entirely possible. And with an acquisitive psychological acumen and an adaptive M.O., all life items remain both legitimate and capably viable.

Of the further pragmatic, I must assert the importance of medication over the course of my schizophrenia. Without meds, psychosis prevails. Initially, symptoms greet with a casualness, but then follows the attack. Psychological warfare declares. I carry no favor for this fete de complete and rather prefer cogito diplomatic. Therefore, I imbibe my meds and get on with it altogether. To the pioneers before, on all sides of the medication paragon (developers and subjects), I again give pause in recognition. Only by modern science comes such compensation. Without medication, my mind shatters and my life scatters. Lucid becomes anomaly and horror the norm. This proffers absent of hyperbole. To the pioneers comes my proclamation, "it is on your sweated brow that comes my now." I thank you.

Lastly of the pragmatics, I would like to briefly describe my protective factors. A "protective factor" is the aggrandized psychological term for things that assist and console. For example, as capitulated, medication and its efficacies is a primary protective factor. Another I have detailed is that of insight and this too is a primary protective factor. My family relationships are also protective. If not for supportive family intervention, my adversities further pile. I often think of my familial good fortune and recognize many are not so lucky. For those lacking family and feeling alone, please know community exists beyond the unit of family. I know schizophrenia and the lone soldier to be a poor prognostic. Please seek alternative support, and know it resides. I assure, if sought, it will be found.

Nearing textual resolution and now of an ideational culmination, I find it most timely to return from whence I began and to capitulate of my first premise. If you recall, my dear reader, at once I offered the contrarian global assertion regarding the typical constitutes to each, and to us all. My offering was the premise of a presenting 10:1 approximate ratio of ingredient "existential fixation" versus ingredient "existential liberation." Such a psychological profile runs uniquely polar to the typical expressions that dominate the current canon. Modern psychology interminably heralds attitudinal capacitation, while all but ignoring the imposed fixational. I find this but a grand intellectual scotoma, and distortion, and I find requisite need for considerable realignment to a more realistic tipping scale.

I have defined existential fixation; namely, characteristics imposed to each. Such designations occupy beyond any means of personal choice, and emerge by manner of creational imposition, and existential vagary. I conceive this realm to be nine-tenths of the life equation. Leaving mathematics proper, therefore, the remains of the quotient assumes as but a sliver to the whole. But let's not be hasty, altogether, to reduce by absolution. After all, a sliver is not nil, and inherency yet remains.

It is now time to drink from the waters of attitudinal disposition. I have led my horse to vast water by recognizance of existential fixation, and now he drinks, but solely from its modest and adjacent puddle. Exclusive to the realm of existential fixation resides the realm of psychological liberation. Its presence exerts by choice and attitude. It therefore begs, given such liberated means, what are the rotund and lineal to do with such capacitation for personal influence? But whoa is me, and whoa is me again! Before launching into a lengthy exposition, I rather prefer to short-circuit this process with an assured acknowledgment that you, my dear reader, already know the rest of this familiar fable. So with reliance on your innate acumen, and by fashion of a curt testimony, I proffer the characteristic remains are but the pertinence of positive countenance.

The value of "positive thinking" currently consumes the modern pop psychology canon. Having a "positive attitude" frequently projects as its panacea. I find this vigorously nauseating. In addition to my induced vertigo (lest we forget our humor, my dear reader), the premise of a good attitude I find to be banal among us. I also find such voluminous reiteration to be most unnecessary. We get it already, and further we do not need instructions! I just find it all too mundane with equal parts balderdash.

Life is intended to be endured not enjoyed. I know all too well that suffering is the true metaphysics. I think this to be a sublimated known to most but yet lacking attentive psychological acknowledgment. Further, if one acknowledges suffering as the primary metaphysical phenomenon, it is likely to be psychologically peripheralized rather than psychologically integrated. And ultimately, if suffering by routine is psychologically integrated, it remains a most stubborn and perfunctory admittance. But with acknowledgment, integration, and admittance, suffering as the true metaphysics can climatically come with a sense of reposeful acceptance. And with such an acceptance, reality's teeth can finally come to bear.

Suffering does not have to be judged as entirely adverse. From the seeds of psychological adversity often blossoms an altruistic and empathic soul. Additionally, I am not expressing that enjoyable times are altogether absent. Let me not be misconstrued for life often comes with a happy countenance and with a lighted frivolity. But I proffer such experiences as more adjunct to the "real deal" of our daily pangs.

Intuition kicks at my ribs that my purviews on remaining positive are likely similar in kind to yours. I find the counsel of "staying positive" as inherently trite and amply lacking in conceptual sophistication. We all know the value of a positive countenance absent of any such psychological admonishments. But although reductionally simplistic and characteristically banal, maintaining a proper attitudinal disposition can at times be a valuable life pragmatic. So with that understanding allow me to explain in brevity of my personal attitudinal dispositions.

I begin with the given of my life as lived with schizophrenia. It is of this primary existential fixation that I will detail my derivative attitudinal reserves. Privy to the charms of my psychological manipulations, exists an attitude of persistence pointed in the direction of employment, leisure, and relationships. This attitudinal quality of persistence has developed over the course of the illness. I regress in my symptoms at times, but I persist in attitude. And when things do not go well or according to plan, I don't care so much. This has been learned through trial and error. The great diplomat Henry **Kissinger** once said, "success is the ability to go from one failure to the next without any loss of enthusiasm." This sentiment has been steeped in to my spiritual aquifer and is a wisdom I often tap as resource. If things don't go well and my effort was earnest, then let the chips fall as they may. I can control my effort but not always the intended outcome.

Within the realm of attitudinal disposition certain variables and resources abound. Inherent to this realm are such wild cards as attitude, belief, conviction, effort, education (both formal and self-taught with the latter being the far more productive and valuable), diligence, interest, and decision-making. Accordingly, faith discerned too belies. Such ethereal distinctions potentiate by a broad spectral appeal, including beyond the singular notion of a Godly ontology.

It is within this realm of psychological liberation, as coupled with existential fixation, that personal destiny is both found and forged. The ever-evolving admixtures of attitude with fixation become the temporal ensemble to one's own personal polka. And Lord knows, with one passing glance to the dance floor it is quickly discerned that we all move and groove to the common vibe but by manner of a singular kinetic. And by such singularity, a life portrays with attributable signature.

But in regard to the remains of the remains and ultimate sentiment, I offer the following. Per the attitudinal, my psychological shelter and philosophical umbrella entails living the leap of faith. Such a characteristic comes by attitude and behavior in concert with conquering schizophrenia. But further yet, this inherited philosophical motto of mine steams like a hot kettle of personal wisdom and pours a tasteful tea of a spiritual imbibe. My leap of faith has become a quantifiable value. It implores to evaluate if I am enthusiastic or cynical, optimistic or pessimistic, and most significantly whether I am lighted by faith or darkened by doubt. In the least, it requires of me a dutiful hope without pardon for a lazy spiritual apathy. At all times, faith may be a difficult proposition; but hope? It indeed springs eternal.

My dear reader, I have now completed my literary task from genesis to coda, and with it comes contented deep breath and relaxing exhalation. The only remains are a most fond farewell from your good company. I have been so fortunate in this written endeavor as it has been a most unexpected existential joy. I remain perplexed by its felt compulsion but after reams of written pages my thoughts have now extinguished. Over the many months, I learned so much, and it was elaborately fun. I had not anticipated the required patience and persistence. Much of what I wrote was highly personal, especially my issues with psychosis. I hope it is realized that "psychosis" does not equate to a permanent craze. Even those with psychosis have their moments of clarity, so please take heart. As for God, I wish you the best in this most personal of issues in whatever you decide. I think divinity is a question we all consider and oftentimes with diverse conclusion. So good luck with your God inquiries and explorations including the foundational issue of belief or non-belief. And lastly, my dear reader, I ask but one last question with the utmost of curiosity as to your response. How are you doing with your own personal leap of faith towards this experience we call life? I hope it is able, if not robust. If amid personal struggle, please remind, hope is always resourceful and is the instigate to faith. But as for now, we must part. But please take heed for parting does not suggest separation. As such, until the time of our clarion communion, I well-wish a cheerful heart, a serene mind, and a joyful countenance. May your life leap in all its realms, may you find your elusive grail, and may you arrive with safe destiny. Fond travels, my beloved.

Glossary

My dear reader:

I have included an adjunct glossary of terms to the text of *On Conquering Schizophrenia* for the purpose of clarity. The terms in this glossary are self-defined and are not verbatim from the dictionary or from other sources. As such, the definitions portray **my** intended meaning as parlance to **your understanding**. I hope you find your glossary experience assistive. Please imbibe and digest as needed!

The bolded words in the text can be found in alphabetical order in the glossary. For ease of read, I bolded the glossary items only upon initial text occurrence rather than every time present.

Amotivation: a psychiatric symptom characterized by a lack of goal-directed behavior.

Anosognosia: a clinical term indicating a lack of prevailing insight into one's mental illness, usually in pertinence to the schizophrenia diagnostic.

Antisocial personality disorder: a psychiatric diagnosis indicating an individual with a temporal pattern of behavior causing undue harm-to-others by variable means, including aggression and/or manipulation. Such individuals are usually considered to have little to no capacitation for empathy towards others i.e. grossly unconscionable.

Aristotle: renowned Greek philosopher (384-322 BC).

Auditory hallucination: a psychiatric symptom indicating the presence of voices heard by an individual that are absent to others and heard singularly. Such hallucinations often are causal of emotional distress.

Best practice: a term used to describe the best typical clinical intervention to a specified diagnostic. Such interventions have been research-tested and confirmed as effective.

Bradford: a philosophy professor, circa 1993, at Geneseo State University.

Buddha: a renowned Eastern philosopher and sage (480-400 BC) whose intellectual canon spurned the teachings of Buddhism.

Camus: renowned French existential philosopher (1913-1960).

Catatonic behavior: behavior characterized by a hyperbolic lack of physical movement.

Chi: an Eastern term referring to a universal and/or personal typical form of "energy." Usually used in a spiritual sense.

Command auditory hallucination: a psychiatric symptom indicating a specified type of auditory hallucination with characteristic impelled directives.

Concept: a specified intellectual idea or construct.

Conduct disorder: a clinical diagnosis indicating a temporal pattern of socially maladaptive, and perhaps unlawful, behavior. Usually used as a precursor diagnostic to an eventual antisocial personality disorder diagnostic.

Continuing Day Treatment (CDT): a modality of formalized mental health care treatment that provided services Monday through Friday with morning hours to afternoon hours. The services included daily "classes," socialization opportunities, meals, and generalized therapy. This modality has recently been discontinued in favor of a similar but differentiated form of treatment referred to as PROS (Personalized Recovery Oriented Services).

Delusion: a psychiatric symptom indicating a "false belief." Delusions can be clinically differentiated according to thematic type. A delusion entails thought content that is personally believed but is highly irrational (and likely impossible) to rational others.

Descartes: renowned French philosopher (1596-1650) known for his ontology, philosophical methodology (involving procedural doubt), and famed first premise of "I think, I am."

DSM: the acronym for the Diagnostic and Statistical Manual of Mental Disorders. The DSM is dedicated to the identification and criteria of all the various conceived mental health diagnostics. The DSM is currently in its fifth edition.

Dysphoric: a psychiatric term indicating a significant emotional disturbance with a characteristic severe depression.

Dystonic: a psychiatric term referencing the acute cognitive status of a prevailing disagreeable idea to one's own intellect. Typically infers an emotionally disturbed status.

Einstein: iconic German born physicist and metaphysicist (1879-1955). Won the Nobel prize for physics in 1921.

Erotomanic delusion: a specified type of delusion, or false belief, involving a believed romantic-type relationship. The other is often conceived as a celebrity or the famed.

Epistemology: the branch of philosophy concerned with "knowledge," of the highest order.

Eugenics: the belief in the superiority of a specified demographic. Usually construed linguistically as a form of racism (as was practiced in Nazi Germany).

Euthymia/euthymic: a psychiatric term indicating a characteristically neutral mood.

Ex nihilo: a Latin term translated to mean "from nothing" or "out of nothing."

Existential fixation: an imposed life item absent of any personal choosing (for example, race, family of origin, birthplace, attributable organicity, gender).

Extreme skepticism: a specified canon of philosophy characterized by a thorough and extreme metaphysical dubiousness.

Flat affect: a psychiatric presentation or appearance inferring a persistently depressed, or quasi-depressed, emotional climate; highly correlated with the schizophrenia diagnostic and classified as a "negative" symptom.

First onset of psychosis: a psychiatric phrasing indicating the first temporal episode(s) of psychosis.

"Forms": a term used by Plato, the renowned Greek philosopher, to indicate his ascertained life ideals; Plato viewed his idyllic forms to be intangible and immutable.

Frankl: renowned author and Holocaust survivor (1905-1997). His authorship was contributory to the annals of psychology.

Gestalt: a clinical and psychological term descriptive of looking at the pieces to the life whole, but with an emphasis and focus on the greater whole. The whole is considered greater than the sum of its parts.

"Goldbergian": an idiom connoting a superfluous and/or elaborate mechanical assemblage for but a simple or rudimentary mechanical result. As derived from the work of the prolific Rube Goldberg (1883-1970), an American cartoonist, author, and inventor.

Harm-to-self/harm-to-others: a psychiatric phrasing privy to clinical safety conception, classification, and consideration.

Kissinger: a former U.S. Secretary of State and American diplomat (1923-). Won the 1973 Nobel Peace Prize.

Ideas of reference: a specified type of delusion when unrelated and innocuous events come with perceptions of association and pertinence, and are experienced as psychologically disturbing.

Hume: renowned Scottish philosopher (1711–1776).

"I have a dream": as spoken by Martin Luther King Jr. in his famous speech (1963).

"I think, I am": a first premise from Rene Descartes's generalized philosophy.

Incongruent affect: a psychiatric symptom indicating an irrational correlation, or a mismatch, between one's mood and one's thought or speech. Indicative of one's cognitive status and found primarily in those with thought disorders.

Infinite regress: a logical pattern and/or logical fallacy typified by an unresolvable recession into an everlasting infinitude.

Kierkegaard: renowned Danish philosopher and theologian (1813-1855) whose writings were a precursor to the philosophical and psychological realms known as "existentialism." The concept of a "leap of faith" is often attributed to Kierkegaard.

"Leap of faith": a specified phrasing most oft attributed to Soren Kierkegaard.

Lilliputians: tiny characters in the classic novel *Gulliver's Travels*, authored in 1726, by Jonathan Swift.

Man's Search for Meaning: classic nonfiction book by Victor Frankl, authored in 1946, detailing his Holocaust experience and survival. Frankl's book was a precursor and instigate to the realm of positive psychology.

Metaphysics: the philosophical or scientific study of reality, or the concept of reality.

Mind-reading: a psychiatric symptom characterized by the delusional belief that one can directly communicate with others by means of mind-to-mind exchanges (without need for overt speech); such exchanges are believed capable irrespective of spatial proximity.

MSW: acronym for the graduate degree of a Master of Social Work.

Narcissistic personality disorder: a psychiatric diagnosis referencing an individual with an established behavioral pattern over time suggestive to the held belief of a personal innate superiority in relation to others. Such individuals are usually thought to have little to no capacitation for empathy towards others and often have a typical characteristic anger otherwise termed as a "narcissistic rage."

Narrative therapy: a psychotherapy modality that focuses on the "story" or the "narrative" of one's life.

Negative symptoms: a psychiatric term indicating a group of symptoms often found in a "schizo" disorder (or thought disorder).

Nietzsche: renowned German philosopher (1844-1900). Known for his controversial proclamation of "God is dead."

Nihilistic (nihilism): the reduction of a theory or concept to a "null" status or "nothing" status. Carries the connotation of a destruction of sorts.

No Exit: a renowned French play written in 1944 by John Paul Sartre (1905-1980) depicting three characters in an interminable hellish context.

Of Mice and Men: classic novel by John Steinbeck first published in 1937.

Ontology: one of the three primary branches of philosophy; specified to the study of "existence."

Pathology: a clinical, psychiatric, and/or medical term indicating "sickness" or "illness."

"Perception is reality": the philosophic conclusion posited by renowned Scottish philosopher David Hume (1711-1776) as translated from its original "esse est percipi."

Personality disorder: a categorical psychiatric diagnostic, inclusive of ten differentiated subtypes, indicating a pattern of persistent dysfunctional behavior over time and variable context.

Philosophical skepticism: philosophical theory or purview characterized by a thorough prevailing dubiousness, or of a thorough doubtfulness. Usually indicates the purview of knowing "nothing to be true," or the void of any knowledge beyond a prevailing doubt.

Plato's idea of the cave: an allegorical idea from philosopher Plato. Being present in the cave allegorically represents being in a cognitive "darkness." Plato's idea of the cave was the contrast to his idyllic (lighted) "forms."

Plato's ideals: Plato's most esteemed life values and virtues; he found them absolute and immutable.

Positive psychology: a psychological canon and talk-therapy modality with a focus on the attitudinal i.e. a positive attitude.

Poverty of thought: a psychiatric symptom indicating the lack of a normalized quantity of thought over time i.e. few thoughts over time.

Poverty of speech: a psychiatric symptom indicating the lack of a normalized quantity of speech over time i.e. markedly minimal verbalizations.

Prima facie: Latin term translated to mean "at first look," superficially, or on the surface of things.

Protective factor: a psychology term referencing life items that promote personal well-being and/or protect one from undue affliction or adversity.

Psychoeducation: a psychology term referencing the clinical methodology of providing education concerning one's mental illness or psychiatric diagnostic(s).

Psychotherapy: a psychology term akin in meaning to "talk-therapy."

Quantum worldview: a primary modern-day scientific and metaphysical purview with characteristic "possibilities" rather than "certainties."

Religious ideation: a psychiatric symptom indicating the presence of ideas or notions with typical religious or spiritual themes and/or overtones.

Romans 5:3-5: a Biblical passage from the book of "Letters to the Romans" that reads, "affliction produces endurance, and endurance, proven character, and proven character, hope, and hope does not disappoint."

SAG: acronym for the Screen Actors Guild, a union organization for actors/performers.

Schizophrenia, paranoid type: a specified primary thought disorder diagnostic with the common symptoms of auditory hallucinations, delusions, and paranoia. Additionally, schizophrenia presents with mixed conglomerates of "positive" and "negative" symptoms. "Paranoid type" further differentiates and specifies from the more generalized schizophrenia conceptualization.

Scotoma: a term indicating a "blind spot." Often used in a psychological sense.

Self-dialoguing: a psychiatric symptom indicating the behavioral phenomenon of talking aloud to oneself usually in response to auditory hallucinations and/or delusions.

Semiotic: term used to connote "meaning" especially as conveyed via a specified medium, i.e., TV, literary, film, music.

Sisyphus: a character of Greek mythology sentenced by punishment to pushing a boulder up a steep incline and once reaching the top only for the boulder to roll back down to its original starting point. Then, Sisyphus would have to repeat this process and was sentenced to do so for all eternity.

Socially constructed reality: a conceptual phrasing indicating the primacy of interpersonal relationships as the characteristic ground or foundation to the shared and common reality.

Sociopath: a psychological term referencing individuals with characteristically low to no empathy and thus prone to violence and antisocial acts.

Solipsistic: a philosophy term indicating the reduction of all items as necessarily nothing beyond the contents and confines of one's mind, i.e., "it's all in your head" (in a most literal sense).

Suicidal gesture: a clinical term indicating an intentional self-harm behavior that deliberately falls short of lethality (suicide). Clinically indicative of psychological disturbance.

Suicidal ideation: a clinical term indicating personal thoughts of wanting to die by method of self-infliction (suicide). Suicidal "ideation" is a clinical distinction from the related concepts of suicidal "intent" and/or suicidal "plan."

Suicidal intent: a clinical term indicating an individual with an active typical attitude (of intent) to complete suicide. Moves well beyond the danger of the singularly specified ideational.

Suicidal plan: a clinical term indicating a chosen method or means for suicide, i.e., by overdose, firearm, hanging, etc.

Tabula rasa: a Latin term translated to mean a "clean slate." Used at times to qualitatively reference a state of mind.

Tacit agreement: a socio-political term indicating unspoken, or unsaid, typical agreements between societal members in regard to mutually expectant societal and/or interpersonal conduct.

Tao: a philosophical and/or spiritual term meaning "the way," the path, or by a specified accordance.

"The ghost in the machine": an idiom used to indicate a lack of knowledge regarding the inner workings of a specified system; oft used in reference to mechanical, psychological, and metaphysical considerations.

The sacred and the profane: a vernacular phrasing referring to the spectral polarities of the sublime versus the vulgar.

The Shawshank Redemption: a 1994 film directed by Frank Darabont detailing the prison life of its protagonist. The film was nominated for seven Academy Awards (but yielded none).

Theological metaphysics: the search for, or study of, reality via a religious or spiritual perspective.

Theory of everything: a vernacular phrasing used to indicate the ultimate theoretical understanding to all metaphysical considerations. Usually thought of as one coherent theory that explains all the vast workings of the universe in all its various capacitations. Such a theory has not yet been achieved and is often perceived as a scientific grail.

Thought blocking: a psychiatric symptom indicating the lack of a normalized succession to one's thoughts.

Thought broadcasting: a psychiatric symptom characterized by the delusional belief that one's thoughts are being projected into the environment and heard verbatim by others.

Thought disorder: a generalized psychiatric categorization and moniker indicating a specified set of diagnostics i.e. schizophrenia and its related.

Transcendental metaphysical ideal: an author coined term indicating a superlative idea or concept that solves ostensible irreconcilable paradox (or opposing dualistic binaries).

"Two and not one": a vernacular phrasing indicating a logical differentiation. Characteristically indicates the presence of two distinct concepts rather than a singular concept. Such a differentiation lends to logical and conceptual clarity.

Wright: an American born stand-up comedian (1955-) known for his comedic deadpan style of delivery.

Zen: a derivative Eastern philosophy with the primary purview of life, or of one's existence, as being inherently and significantly paradoxical.